ACCORDING

to Promise

Register This New Book

Benefits of Registering*

- ✓ FREE **replacements** of lost or damaged books

- ✓ FREE **audiobook** – *Pilgrim's Progress,*
  audiobook edition

- ✓ FREE information about new titles
  and other **freebies**

www.anekopress.com/new-book-registration

*See our website for requirements and limitations.

ACCORDING

to Promise

Of Salvation, Life, and Eternity

*Or, The Lord's Method of Dealing
with His Chosen People*

Charles H. Spurgeon

We love hearing from our readers. Please contact us at www.anekopress.com/questions-comments with any questions, comments, or suggestions.

According to Promise – Charles H. Spurgeon
Revised Edition Copyright © 2017

All rights reserved. No part of this book may be reproduced, stored in a retrieval system, or transmitted in any form or by any means – electronic, mechanical, photocopying, recording, or otherwise, without written permission from the publisher.

Unless otherwise marked, scripture quotations are taken from the Jubilee Bible, copyright © 2000, 2001, 2010, 2013 by Life Sentence Publishing, Inc. Used by permission of Life Sentence Publishing, Inc., Abbotsford, Wisconsin. All rights reserved.

Cover Design: Jonathan Lewis
Editors: Paul Miller and Ruth Zetek

Aneko Press

www.anekopress.com

Aneko Press, Life Sentence Publishing, and our logos are trademarks of Life Sentence Publishing, Inc.
203 E. Birch Street
P.O. Box 652
Abbotsford, WI 54405

RELIGION / Christian Life / Spiritual Growth

Paperback ISBN: 978-1-62245-635-2

eBook ISBN: 978-1-62245-636-9

10 9 8 7 6 5 4 3 2

Available where books are sold

Contents

Chapter 1

A Spiritual Analysis

Examine me, O LORD and prove me; melt my kidneys and my heart. (Psalm 26:2)

It is very important to be able to distinguish between things that are different, because we cannot always rely upon appearances. Things which seem to be alike may still be the opposite of each other. A scorpion may be like an egg, and a stone may be like a piece of bread, but they are far from being the same. Like may be very unlike. This is especially the case in spiritual things, and therefore it requires us to be on our guard.

People can be very religious and yet still die in their sins. They may look very much like children of God and yet still be children of wrath. Many unconverted people have beliefs which are similar to true biblical faith, and yet they do not have true faith. Certain people exhibit religious feelings which have the warmth of spiritual love, but are quite empty of God's grace. Every grace can be counterfeited, even as jewels can be imitated. As glass gems are wonderfully like the real stones, so imitation graces are marvelously like the work of the Spirit of God. In matters of the soul, a man will need to have all his sense about him, or he will soon deceive his own heart. It is to be feared that many are already mistaken and will never discover their delusion until they open their eyes in the eternal world, where they will indeed face terrible disappointment.

A child dead in sin due to his sinful human nature may be carefully washed by his mother, but this will not make the child a living child of grace. The life of God within the soul creates an infinite difference between the person who has it and the one who does not; the point is to make sure that we have this life.

Are YOU sure that you have it? Are YOU sure that you have Him?

It will be an awful thing to cry, *Peace, peace; when there is no peace* (Jeremiah 6:14). It would be terrible to prophesy smooth things for yourself, to make your heart at ease, to lull your conscience to slumber, and to never wake out of sleep until the sound of the thunder of judgment startles you out of presumption and into endless horror.

I desire to help you examine yourself spiritually. I want you to go further than examination, though, and attain such abundance of grace that your holy and happy condition will become a witness to yourself.

The first part of this little book is meant to be a sieve to separate the chaff from the wheat. Use it on your own soul. It may be the most profitable and beneficial work you have ever done. He who looked into his accounts and found that his business was losing money was saved from bankruptcy. This may happen also to you. If, however, you discover that your heavenly business is prospering, it will be a great comfort to you. You cannot lose by honestly searching your own heart.

Friend, try it at once.

Chapter 2

Natural vs. Supernatural

*For it is written that Abraham had two sons,
the one by a bondmaid, the other by a freewoman. But he who was of the bondwoman
was born according to the flesh, but he of the
freewoman was born through the promise.*
(Galatians 4:22-23)

Abraham had two sons. Ishmael and Isaac were
beyond all dispute genuine sons of Abraham.
Yet one of them inherited the covenant blessing, while
the other was simply a prosperous man of the world.
See how close together these two were! They were born
in the same society, called the same great patriarch
"father," and traveled in the same encampment with
him. Yet Ishmael was a stranger to the covenant, while
Isaac was the heir of the promise. How little value there
is in blood and birth!

A more remarkable instance than this happened

a little afterwards. Esau and Jacob were born of the same mother at the same birth, yet it is written, *Jacob have I loved, but Esau have I hated* (Romans 9:13). One became gracious, and the other profane. Two people may be closely together, and yet they can be widely separated! Truly, it is not only that *there shall be two men in one bed: the one shall be taken, and the other shall be left* (Luke 17:34), but it is also true that two will come into the world at the same moment, and yet one of them will take up his inheritance with God, and the other will sell his birthright for a morsel of meat. We may be in the same church with others, baptized in the same water, seated at the same communion table, singing the same psalm, and offering the same prayer, and yet we may be of two different cultures as different as the offspring of the woman are from the offspring of the Serpent.

Abraham's two sons are declared by Paul to be the types of two tribes of men who are much alike, and yet widely differ. They are unlike in their origin. They were both sons of Abraham, but Ishmael, the child of Hagar, was the offspring of Abraham under ordinary conditions. He was born after the flesh. Isaac, the son of Sarah, was not born by the strength of nature, for his father was more than a hundred years old, and his mother was long past childbearing age. He was given to his parents by the Lord, and was born according to *the promise* through faith. This is a critical distinction, and it distinguishes the true child of God from him who only claims to be a child of God. The promise lies at the bottom of the distinction, and the power which goes to accomplish the promise creates and maintains the difference. Therefore, the promise, which is our inheritance, is also our test and benchmark.

Let us use the test at once by seeing whether the power which fulfills the promise has worked in us. Let me ask a few questions: How were you converted? Was it by yourself, by the persuasion of men, by carnal excitement – or was it by the working of the Spirit of God? You profess to have been born again. From where did that new birth come? Did it come from God in consequence of His eternal purpose and promise, or did it come out of yourself? Was it your old nature trying to do better and working itself up to its best form? If so, you are Ishmael.

If you began in the flesh and have continued in the flesh, you will die in the flesh.

Instead, was it that you, being spiritually dead and having no strength whatsoever to rise out of your lost condition, were visited by the Spirit of God who put forth His divine energy and caused life from heaven to enter into you? Then you are Isaac.

All will depend upon the beginning of your spiritual life and the source from which that life at first began. If you began in the flesh and have continued in the flesh, you will die in the flesh.

Have you never read John 3:6: *That which is born of the flesh is flesh*? Before long, the flesh will perish, and from it you will reap corruption. Only *that which is born of the Spirit is spirit*; the joy is that the spirit will live, and from that you will reap life everlasting. Whether you profess to be a Christian or not, I urge you to ask yourself: *Have I felt the power of the Spirit of God?*

Is the life that is within you the result of the turmoil of your own natural desires, or is it something new, infused, imparted, and implanted from above? Is your spiritual life a heavenly creation? Have you been created anew in Christ Jesus? Have you been born again by divine power?

Ordinary religion is human nature dressed up with a thin layer of what is thought to be grace. Sinners have polished themselves up and brushed off the worst of the rust and the filth, and they think their old nature is as good as new. This touching up and repairing of the old nature is all very well, but it falls short of what is needed. You may wash the face and hands of Ishmael as much as you please, but you cannot turn him into Isaac. You may improve your human nature, and the more you do so the better it is for certain temporary purposes; but you cannot change it into grace. There is a distinction at the very source between the stream which rises in the bog of fallen humanity and the river which proceeds from the throne of God.

Do not forget that our Lord Himself said, *Ye must be born again* (John 3:7). If you have not been born again from above, all your church or chapel attendance means nothing. Your prayers and your tears, your Bible readings, and all that have come only from yourself, can only lead to yourself. Water will naturally rise as high as its source, but no higher. That which begins with human nature will rise to human nature, but it cannot reach to the divine nature. Was your new birth natural or supernatural? Was it of the will of man or of God? Was it something you did in your religion, or was it something that God did in you? Much will depend upon your answer to that question.

Between the true child of God and the mere professor of Christianity, there is a most serious distinction as to origin. Isaac was born *according to the promise.* Ishmael was not of the promise, but was of the course of nature. Where nature's strength suffices, there is no promise; but when human energy fails, the word of the Lord comes in. God had said that Abraham would have a son of Sarah. Abraham believed God's promise and rejoiced in it. Isaac was born as the result of the divine promise, by the power of God. There could have been no Isaac if there had been no promise, and there can be no true believer apart from the promise of grace and the grace of the promise.

Let me now inquire as to your salvation. Are you saved by what you have done? Is your religion the product of your own natural strength? Do you feel able to achieve everything that salvation may require? Do you conclude yourself to be in a safe and happy condition because of your natural excellence and moral ability? Then you take after the manner of Ishmael, and the inheritance will not come to you, for it is not an inheritance according to the flesh, but according to the promise.

On the other hand, you might say something like this: "My hope lies only in the promise of God. He has set forth that promise in the person of His Son, Jesus, to every sinner who believes in Him. I do believe in

Him; therefore, I trust and believe that the Lord will fulfill His promise and bless me. I look for heavenly blessedness, not as the result of my own efforts, but as the gift of God's free favor. My hope is set only and completely upon the free and gratuitous love of God to guilty men, by which He has given His Son, Jesus Christ, to put away sin and to bring in everlasting righteousness for those who do not deserve it." If you speak from the heart like this, then this is a different kind of language from that of the Ishmaelites, who say, *We have Abraham as our father* (Matthew 3:9). You have now learned to speak as Isaac speaks.

The difference may seem small to the careless, but it is great indeed. Hagar, the slave-mother, is a very different person from Sarah, the princess. To the one there is no covenant promise; to the other the blessing belongs forevermore. Salvation by works is one thing; salvation by grace is another. Salvation by human strength is the opposite of salvation by divine power. Salvation by our own resolve is the opposite of salvation by the promise of God.

Put yourself under this inquiry and see to which family you belong. *Are you of Ishmael or of Isaac?*

If you find that you are like Isaac, born according to the promise, remember that your name means "laughter," for that is the interpretation of the Hebrew name *Isaac.* Take care that you rejoice with joy unspeakable and full of glory. Your new birth is a wonderful thing. If both Abraham and Sarah laughed at the thought of Isaac, you may certainly do so concerning yourself. There are times when, if I sit alone and think of the grace of God to me, the most undeserving of all His creatures, I am ready to laugh and cry at the same time for joy that the Lord should have ever looked in love and favor upon me. Yes, and every child of God must have felt the working of that Isaac nature within his soul, filling his mouth with laughter, because the Lord has done great things for him.

Notice carefully the difference between the two off-spring from their very beginning. Ishmael comes of man, and by man. Isaac comes *by God's promise.* Ishmael is the child of Abraham's flesh. Isaac is Abraham's child too, but then the power of God comes in, and from the weakness of his parents it is made clear that Isaac is of the Lord – a gift according to promise. True faith is certainly the act

> The Lord our God, who instructs us to believe, also enables us to believe.

of the one who believes, and true repentance is the act of the one who repents; yet both faith and repentance may with unquestionable certainty be described as the work of God, even as Isaac is the son of Abraham and Sarah, and yet he is still more the gift of God. The Lord our God, who instructs us to believe, also enables us to believe. All that we do that is acceptable to God is because the Lord works it in us; yes, the very desire to do it is of His working. No religion is worth one cent that is not essentially the outflow of man's own heart, and yet it must be beyond question the work of the Holy Spirit who dwells within him.

O friend, if what you have within you is natural, and only natural, it will not save you! The inward work must be supernatural. It must come from God, or it will miss the covenant blessing. A life of grace will be your own, even as Isaac was truly the child of Abraham; but still more it will be of God, for salvation is of the Lord. We must be born from above. Concerning all our religious feelings and actions, we must be able to say, "Lord, You have worked all our works in us."

Chapter 3

Two Kinds of Life

Neither, because they are the seed of Abraham, are all sons, but, In Isaac shall thy seed be called. That is, Those who are sons of the flesh, these are not the sons of God; but those who are sons of the promise are counted in the generation. For the word of the promise is this, At this time I will come, and Sara shall have a son. (Romans 9:7-9)

Ishmael and Isaac differed as to origin, and so there was a difference in their nature which showed itself in their lives, and was mainly seen in their relation to *the promise.*

According to the birth, so will be the life which comes from it. In the case of the man who is only what he made himself to be, there will be only what nature gives him; but in the case of the man who is created anew by the Spirit of God, there will be signs following. *But of him ye are reborn in Christ Jesus, who of God is made unto us wisdom and righteousness and sanctification and redemption, that, according as it is written, He that glories, let him glory in the Lord* (1 Corinthians 1:30-31).

There will be in the born-again man that which the new life brings with it; in the natural man there will be nothing of the kind.

Ishmael exhibited certain natural characteristics of Abraham along with some natural characteristics of his slave-mother. He was a princely man like his father, and he inherited the patriarch's noble bearing; but Isaac had the faith of his father, and was in the succession as to a holy, inward spiritual life. As the heir of the promise, Isaac remained with his father, Abraham, while Ishmael formed camps of his own in the wilderness. Isaac sought a companion from his ancestral lineage in Mesopotamia, but Ishmael's mother took for him a wife out of Egypt, which was very natural, since she came from Egypt herself. We tend to prefer that which is familiar and comfortable to us.

Isaac meditated in the field in the evening, for his life was filled with things of God; but Ishmael contended with all who showed up, for he cared for earthly things. Meditation is not for the wild man whose hand is against every man and every man's hand against him. Isaac surrendered himself as a sacrifice to God, but you see nothing like that in Ishmael. Self-sacrifice is not for Ishmael; rather, he is a killer and a murderer instead of a lamb that presents itself to God.

You will find that if you are religiously trained

and taught and become "pious," as they call it, yet are not renewed in heart nor changed by the Holy Spirit, you will not live the life of a true child of God. You may display many of the outward characteristics of a Christian. You may be able to sing and pray and quote some Scripture, and maybe even tell a little bit about an emotional experience; but you must be born again to know the reality and certainty of the truth

The child of the promise abides with God's people and counts it his privilege to be numbered with them.

of the fellowship of the saints, communion in secret with the living God, and the surrendering of yourself to Him as your reasonable service.

The child of the promise abides with God's people and counts it his privilege to be numbered with them. The child of the promise feels that he is in the best company when no one can see him or be seen by him, but when the almighty God draws near to him and fellowships with him. The child of the promise, and he only, is able to go up to the top of Moriah, there to be bound upon the altar and to yield himself up to God (see Genesis 22). I mean by this, that only he who is born of the Spirit will yield himself wholly to God and will love the Lord better than life itself. Your nature and conduct will be according to your beginning. Therefore, I pray that you may begin right, so that as you profess to be a child of God's kingdom, you may prove to be an actual trueborn heir.

Ishmael, who was born after the flesh, the child of the bondwoman, must always bear the mark of a servant. The child of a slave is not born free. Ishmael was not and could not be what Isaac was – the child of the free woman. Now listen: I don't say that Ishmael ever wanted to be like Isaac. I don't say that he felt himself to be lower than Isaac because he was different from Isaac; but, indeed, he was so. The man who is laboring for self-salvation by his own works, feelings, and self-denials may be proudly ignorant of his condition as a slave. He may even boast that he was born free and was never in bondage to anyone, and yet he spends his whole life in servitude. He never knows what liberty means, what it means to be content, or what delight in God means.

He does not understand when people talk about "full assurance of faith," and he concludes that they must be presumptuous. He has scarcely time to breathe between all his works of the flesh. He has done so much, but he must do so much more. He has suffered so much, but he must suffer so much more. He has never come into the rest which remains for the people of God (Hebrews 4:9), for he is born of the bondwoman, and his spirit is ever in bondage.

On the other hand, he who is born of the free woman and understands that salvation is of the grace of God from beginning to end, and that where God has given His grace, He does not take it back, *for the gifts and calling of God are without repentance* (Romans 11:29) – such a man accepting the finished work of Christ and knowing that he is *accepted in the beloved* (Ephesians 1:6) rests in the Lord and rejoices exceedingly. His life and his spirit are filled with joy and peace, for he was born free and he is free; yes, he is free indeed.

Do you understand the freedom of the child of God, or are you still in servitude under the law, afraid of punishment, afraid of being sent away into the wilderness? Are you free by faith, or are you still depending upon your own works and efforts? If you are depending upon your works, you have not received *the promise*, or you would know that such a thing could not be. To Isaac, the child of the promise, the heritage belongs, and he abides forever without fear of being cast out.

Those who are born as Ishmael was, according to the flesh, and those whose religion is a matter of their own power and strength, are concerned with earthly things, as Ishmael was. Only those who are born from above through the promise according to faith will, like Isaac, care for heavenly things.

The naturally religious man cares for earthly things. He is very regular at his place of worship, but while he is there, he thinks of his business, his house, or his farm. Does he enjoy the worship of God? No! There is a sermon. Does he receive with meekness the engrafted word which is able to save his soul (James 1:21)? No! He criticizes it as if it were a political rant. He gives his money to the cause of God as others do. Of course he does, for he feels that he has to quiet his conscience and keep up his good reputation; but does he care for the glory of God? By no means. If he did, he would give more than money. His heart's prayers would go up for the progress of the kingdom of God. Does he mourn and cry because of the sins of the times? Do you find him alone with God pouring out his heart in anguish because even in his own family there are those who are not converted to God? Did you ever see in him a high and holy joy when sinners are converted – an exultation because the kingdom of Christ is coming? Oh no, he never rises to that.

All the service of God is outward to him. He has never entered into the core and heart of spiritual things, and he never can. The carnal mind, even when it is religious, is still enmity against God; it is not reconciled to God, and indeed cannot be (Romans 8:7). There must be a spiritual mind created in the man. He must become a new creature in Christ Jesus before he can appreciate, understand, and enjoy spiritual things.

> The carnal mind, even when it is religious, is still enmity against God.

To come back to where we started – *Ye must be born again* (John 3:7) – we must be born of the Spirit. We must receive a supernatural life by being made alive from our death in sin. We cannot bear the fruit of the Spirit until we have the inner life of the Spirit. Ishmael will be Ishmael, and Isaac will be Isaac. As the man is, so will his conduct be. The man of sight and reason and human power may do his best as Ishmael did, but only the child of the promise will rise to the life and walk of faith as Isaac did.

"Those are some hard and fast lines," someone says. Sometimes it is a great blessing to have those hard lines drawn, and drawn very straight too. By this means we may be set on the right track for eternity. The other day someone said to a friend of mine, "I once went to hear Mr. Spurgeon, and when I went into the Tabernacle, if you had asked me about myself, I would have said that I was as religious a man as ever lived in Newington, and as good a man, certainly, as was ever part of a congregation; but all this was reversed when I heard the gospel that day. I came out of the place with every feather plucked out of me. I felt myself the most wretched sinner on the face of the earth, and I said I would never go to hear that man again, for he has destroyed me altogether. Yes," he continued, "but that was the best thing that could have happened to me. I was made to look away from myself and all that I could do, and look to God and to His omnipotent grace, and to understand that I must pass under my Creator's hand again, or I could never see His face with joy."

I hope you know this truth for yourself. It is a solemn truth. Even as first of all God made Adam, so He must make us over again, or else we can never bear His image nor behold His glory. We must come under the influence of *the promise* and live upon the promise, or our lives will never be guided by right principles nor directed to right ends.

Chapter 4

Two Kinds of Hope

And as for Ishmael, I have heard thee:
Behold, I shall bless him and will make him
fruitful and will multiply him exceedingly;
he shall beget twelve princes, and I will make
him a great nation. But I will establish my
covenant with Isaac, whom Sarah shall bear
unto thee at this set time in the next year.
(Genesis 17:20-21)

I t is not at all surprising that two people, so different in their birth and nature as Ishmael and Isaac, became very different in their hopes. To Isaac, the covenant promise became the guiding principle of his being; but for Ishmael, no such light had arisen. Ishmael aimed at large things, for he was the natural son of one of the greatest of men; but Isaac looked for still-higher objects, because he was the child of the promise and the inheritor of the covenant of grace which the Lord had made with Abraham.

Ishmael, with his high and daring spirit, looked to begin a nation which would never be subdued, a race untamable as the wild donkey of the desert; and his desire has been abundantly granted. The Bedouin Arabs are to this day true copies of their great ancestor. Ishmael in life and death realized the narrow, earthly hopes for which he looked, but on the list of those who saw the day of Christ and died in the hope of glory, his name is not entered. Isaac, on the other hand, saw far ahead, even to the day of Christ. *He looked for a city which has foundations, whose builder and maker is God* (Hebrews 11:10).

Ishmael, like Passion in *The Pilgrim's Progress*, had his best things here below; but Isaac, like Patience, waited for his best things in the future. His treasures were not in the tent and in the field, but in the *things not seen as yet* (Hebrews 11:7). He had received the great covenant promise, and there he found greater riches than all the flocks of Nebaioth could minister to him. The daystar of promise had shined upon his eye, and he expected a full noon of blessing in the fullness of the appointed time. The promise so operated upon him as to guide the direction of his thoughts and expectations. Is it so with you? Have you received and embraced the promise of eternal life? Are you, therefore, hoping for *things not seen as yet*? Have you an eye to that which none can behold except believers in the faithfulness of God? Have you exchanged the rut of the present perception of your senses for the way of faith in the unseen and eternal?

No doubt the reception of the promise and the enjoyment of its hopes influenced the mind and demeanor of Isaac so that he was of a restful spirit. For him there were no wars and fightings. He yielded the present and waited for the future. Isaac felt that since he was born according to the promise, it was for God to bless him and to fulfill the promise that He had made concerning him, and so he remained with Abraham and kept himself distant from the outside world. He both quietly hoped and patiently waited for the blessing of God. His eye was on the future, on the great nation yet to come, the promised land, and the yet more-glorious promised seed in whom all the nations of the earth would be blessed (Genesis 22:18). For all this, he looked to God alone, wisely judging that He who gave the promise would Himself see to its fulfillment.

> Have you exchanged the rut of the present perception of your senses for the way of faith in the unseen and eternal?

Because of this faith, Isaac was still active, yet he showed none of the proud self-reliance that was so apparent in Ishmael. He was energetic in his own way, with a calm confidence in God and a quiet submission to His supreme will. Year after year, he held on in the separated life and bravely faced the danger unarmed that arose from his heathen neighbors – dangers which Ishmael confronted with his sword and with his bow. Isaac's trust was in that voice that said, *Touch not my anointed, and do my prophets no harm* (1 Chronicles 16:22). He was a man of peace, and yet he lived as securely as his warlike brother. His faith in the promise gave him hope of security, and it gave him security itself, though the Canaanites were still in the land.

The promise affects our present life by creating in us an elevated spirit, a life above visible surroundings, and a calm and heavenly frame of mind. Isaac found his bow and his spear in his God. Yahweh was his shield and his *exceeding great reward* (Genesis 15:1). Without a foot of land to call his own, dwelling as a sojourner and a stranger in the land which God had given him by promise, Isaac was content to live upon the promise and count himself rich in joys to come.

His remarkably quiet and steady spirit, while leading the strange, unearthly life of one of the great Pilgrim Fathers, sprang out of his simple faith in the promise of the unchanging God. Hope, kindled by a divine promise, affects the entire life of a man in his inmost thoughts, ways, and feelings. It may seem to be of less importance than correct moral behavior, but in truth, it is of vital importance, not only in itself, but also in that which it produces upon the mind, heart, and life. The inner hope of a man is a truer test of his condition before God than his actions of any one day, or even the public devotions of a year. Isaac pursued his quiet, holy way until he grew old and blind and gently fell asleep trusting in his God, who had revealed Himself to him and had called him to be His friend. God had said to him, *abide in this land, and I will be with thee, and will bless thee; and in thy seed shall all the Gentiles of the earth* (Genesis 26:3a; 22:18a).

As a man's hopes are, so is he. If his hope is in the promise of God, it is well, and it must be well with him.

What are your hopes? "Well," says someone, "I am waiting until a relative dies, and then I will be rich. I have great expectations." Another person hopes in his steadily growing business. A third person expects much from a promising, risky investment. Hopes that can be realized in a dying world are mere mockeries. Hopes that have no outlook beyond the grave are dim windows for a soul to look through. Happy is he who believes *the promise* and feels assured of its fulfillment to himself in due time, leaving all else in the hands of infinite wisdom and love. Such hope will endure trials, conquer temptations, and enjoy heaven below.

When Christ died on the cross, our hopes began. When He arose, they were confirmed. When He ascended on high, they began to be fulfilled. When He comes a second time, they will be realized. In this world we will have a pilgrim's sustenance and a table spread in the presence of our enemies (Psalm 23:5). In the world to come, we will possess the land which flows with milk and honey, a land of peace and joy, where the sun will no more go down, neither will the moon withdraw itself (Numbers 14:8; Isaiah 60:20). Until then, we hope, and our hope lays hold upon *the promise.*

Chapter 5

Persecution and Children of the Promise

So that we, brethren, as Isaac was, are the children of promise. But as then he that was born according to the flesh persecuted him that was born according to the Spirit, even so it is now. (Galatians 4:28-29)

When brothers differ as much as Ishmael and Isaac, it is not surprising if they disagree and quarrel and indulge unkind feelings. Ishmael was older than Isaac, and when the time came for Isaac to be weaned, his mother, Sarah, saw the son of the bond-woman mocking her child. It was early on in their lives that the difference of birth and condition began to display itself. This may serve to us as an indication of what we may expect if we possess the God-given life and are heirs according to the promise. Those who are under the bondage of the law cannot love those who are freely born by the gospel, and in some way or other they soon display their enmity.

We are not now thinking of the hostility between the wicked world and the church, but of that which exists between men of a merely natural religion and those who are truly born of God. We are not speaking of the Philistines opposing Isaac, but of Isaac's brother, Ishmael, mocking him. Fiercest of all is this opposition of the externally religious toward those who are born from above and worship God in spirit and in truth. Many precious children of God have suffered bitterly from the cruel hatred of those who professed to be their brothers and sisters.

The motive of Ishmael was probably envy. He could not endure that the little one should have preeminence over himself. He seemed to say, "This is the heir, and therefore I hate him." Perhaps he mocked Isaac's position as heir, and boasted that he had as good a right to the estate as ever the child of the promise could have. In the same way, those who are merely religious, those who only profess to be Christians, envy the condition of real believers and consider themselves to be quite as good as the best of those who are saved by the grace of God. They do not desire the grace of God themselves, and yet, like the dog in the manger, they cannot bear that others should have it. They envy the hope in Christ that these true saints have. They envy their peace of mind and their enjoyment of the favor of God. If any of you find it so, do not be in the least surprised.

The envy of Ishmael displayed itself most at the great feast which had been made at his brother's weaning. In the same manner do formalists – those who take pride in their religion and in their own alleged goodness – like the elder brother in the parable, become most provoked when there is most occasion for rejoicing in connection with the Father's beloved child (Luke 15:11-32). The music and dancing of the true family are bitterness and vexation to proud, mere professors of religion who do not know true life in Christ Jesus.

When a person moves from doubt to complete assurance of salvation, and when a person of the world is changed to delight in that which is holy, then the carnal religionist

> **The world mocks saints for weaknesses which in others would be overlooked.**

sneers and calls the godly person insane or fanatical, or murmurs with resentful sarcasm, "Poor fools! Let them alone; they are sadly deluded." People who are religious but not truly regenerated, those who are working and hoping to be saved by their own merits, usually exhibit a bitter hatred towards those who are born of the promise.

Sometimes they mock their feebleness. Maybe Ishmael called Isaac a mere baby, just weaned. Believers are sometimes feeble and exceedingly likely to stir up the derision of those who think themselves to be strong-minded. Isaac could not deny that he was weak, and neither can believers deny that they are faulty and subject to weakness and sin, which may put them under rightful reproof; but the world makes more of this than justice will allow. The world mocks saints for weaknesses which in others would be overlooked. We must not think it a strange thing if our insignificance and imperfection should set proud and self-righteous Pharisees jeering at us and our gospel.

Frequently the jeering is raised because of the believer's assertions. Isaac was called "the heir," and Ishmael could not bear to hear it. "Look," says the legalist, "that man over there was a known sinner not long ago; now he says he has believed in Jesus Christ, and therefore he declares that he knows himself to be saved and accepted and sure of heaven. Did you ever hear of such presumption?" He who hugs his chains hates the presence of a free man. He who refuses the mercy of God because he proudly trusts his own merits is angry with the man who rejoices to be saved by grace.

Perhaps the little Isaac, the child of such aged parents, seemed odd and strange to the young half-bred Egyptian. No person is so much a foreigner to his fellow men as a man born from above. To live by faith upon the promise of God ought to seem the most proper and natural thing in the world, but it is not regarded in this way. On the contrary, people consider those to be strange who believe in God and actually live according to such a belief. Wicked boys in the streets still mock foreigners, and men of the world still mock true believers, simply because of their unworldly spirit and conduct. To us this is a testimony for good, for our Lord said, *If ye were of the world, the world would love its own; but because ye are not of the world, but I have chosen you out of the world, therefore the world hates you* (John 15:19).

In a thousand ways – many of them so petty as to

be unworthy to mention – the believer can be made to experience *cruel mockings* (Hebrews 11:36), and he ought to be prepared to do so. After all, it is but a small matter to be persecuted nowadays, for the fires of Smithfield are quenched, the Lollards' tower contains no prisoners, and not even a thumbscrew remains in use.[1] Courage, good brother! Even though you might be ridiculed, no bones will be broken, and if you are brave enough to despise contempt, not even your sleep will be disturbed.[2]

> No association of the unregenerate with the church of God will avail to alter their nature.

Ishmael's mocking Isaac is only one among ten thousand proofs of the enmity which exists between the offspring of the woman and the offspring of the Serpent. The mixture of these two in Abraham's household came about through his going down into Egypt and acting in an unbelieving manner toward Pharaoh. Then the Egyptian bondwoman was given to Sarah, and the evil element came into the camp. Sarah, in an evil hour, gave the bondwoman to her husband, resulting in sorrow and ten thousand tears.

No association of the unregenerate with the church of God will avail to alter their nature. Ishmael in Abraham's encampment is still Ishmael. Today, the fiercest enemies of the truth of God are the unsaved

---

1   Smithfield was a place where Christians were sometimes martyred; the Lollards were disciples of John Wycliffe and were often persecuted, and the thumbscrew was a method of torture sometimes used against Christians.

2   Christians in the West have been relatively free from persecution for the past couple hundred years, although Christians around the world in many countries are daily tortured and killed for following Jesus. We need to be prepared for such times no matter where we live.

in our communion of saints. These are they who make believers in sound evangelical teaching look like strangers in the churches which were founded on the basis of scriptural doctrine. They make us foreigners in our own land. They are lenient to all manner of heresy, but they mock those who believe in the doctrines of grace as old-fashioned and bigoted – as out-of-date people who ought to willfully seek out graves and bury themselves. Yet the man who trusts his God and believes in His covenant will be able to survive all mockeries, for he counts the reproach of Christ greater riches than all the treasures of Egypt (Hebrews 11:26). It is by no means shameful to trust God; on the contrary, it is a point of honor with good men to trust in Him who is faithful and true, and if they have to suffer for it, they do so joyfully. Clothe yourselves, therefore, with a holy courage, you who are learning through grace to live upon the promise of God by faith. Was not the great Head of the family despised and rejected of men? Must not the rest of the brotherhood be conformed to *the firstborn among many brethren* (Romans 8:29)? If we are made partakers of Christ's sufferings, we will be partakers of His glory (1 Peter 4:13); therefore, let us gladly join with Jesus Christ – the crucified heir of all things.

Chapter 6

Where the Heart Goes We Go

Nevertheless what does the scripture say? Cast out the bondwoman and her son, for the son of the bondwoman shall not be heir with the son of the freewoman. (Galatians 4:30)

I saac and Ishmael lived together for a time. The self-religionist and the believer in *the promise* may be members of the same church for years, but they are not agreed and cannot be happy together, for their principles are essentially opposed. As the believer grows in grace and enters upon his spiritual manhood, he will be more and more disagreeable to the religionist and the legalist, and ultimately the two have no fellowship with one another. They must separate, and this is the word that will be fulfilled to the Ishmaelite: *Cast out this bondwoman and her son; for the son of this bondwoman shall not be heir with my son, even with Isaac* (Genesis 21:10; Galatians 4:30).

Grievous as the parting may be, it will be according to the divine will and according to the necessities of the case. Oil and water will not mingle, and neither will the natural man's religion agree with that which is born of the promise and sustained by the promise. Their parting will be only the outward result of a serious difference which always existed.

Ishmael was sent away, but he soon ceased to regret it, for he found greater freedom with the wild tribes of the country among whom he soon became a great man. He prospered much and became the father of princes. He was in his proper sphere in the wide world. There he had honor and gained a name among its great ones. It often happens that the carnally religious man has many excellent habits and ways about him, and having a desire to shine, he goes into society and is appreciated and becomes notable. The world is sure to love its own. The aspiring religionist usually forsakes his first friends, and openly declares: "I have given up the old-fashioned style of religion. It was fine to hang around true Christians while I was poor, but now that I have made a fortune, I feel that I must mix with a more fashionable set of people." He does so, and he has his reward. Ishmael had his portion in this life and never expressed a desire to share in the heavenly covenant and its mysterious blessings. If you would feel freer and more at home in society than in the church of God, then know assuredly that you belong to the world. Do not deceive yourself. As your heart is, so are you. No amount of force or work can turn Ishmael into Isaac, or a person of the world into an heir of heaven.

Outwardly, and in this present life, the heir of the promise did not appear to have the best of it. Nor, indeed, should this be expected, since they who choose their heritage in the future have, in fact, agreed to accept trials in the present.

Isaac experienced certain afflictions that Ishmael never knew. Isaac was mocked and he was laid on the altar as a sacrifice, but nothing like this happened to Ishmael. You, who like Isaac are the children of the promise, must not envy those who are the heirs of this present life, even though their circumstances might seem easier than your own. Your temptation is to do so, even as the psalmist did when he was grieved because of the prosperity of the wicked (as in Psalm 73). There is in this agonizing a measure of running back from our spiritual choice, but have we not agreed to take our reward in the future rather than in the present? Do we regret the bargain?

You, who like Isaac are the children of the promise, must not envy those who are the heirs of this present life.

Moreover, how absurd it is to envy those who are themselves so much to be pitied! To lose the promise is practically to lose everything, and the self-righteous have lost it. These worldly professors of Christianity have no spiritual light or life, and they desire none. What a loss to be in the dark, to be so spiritually blind, and not to know it! They have enough religion to make them respectable among people and comfortable in their own consciences, but this is an unfortunate gain if they are abominable in the sight of God. They feel no inward fightings and wrestlings. They find no contention of the old man against the new, and so they go through life with a carefree attitude, knowing nothing of the truth until their end comes. What wretchedness to be so deceived! Again, I say, do not envy them. Far better is the life of Isaac with its sacrifice than that of Ishmael with its sovereignty and wild freedom; for all the greatness of those of this world will soon be ended, and they will leave nothing behind but that which will make the eternal world to be the more miserable.

Do not think, though, that true believers are unhappy. If in this life only we had hope, we would be miserable indeed (1 Corinthians 15:19), but *the promise* lights up our whole course of life and makes us truly blessed. God's smile seen by faith gives us fullness of joy. If you put the believer's life at the greatest possible disadvantage, paint it in the darkest colors, take away from it not only comforts but also necessities, even then the Christian at his worst is better than the person of this world at his best.

Let Ishmael have the whole world; yes, give him as many worlds as there are stars in the midnight sky, and we will not envy him. It is our duty still to take up our cross and to be strangers and foreigners with God in this land, as all our fathers in the faith were; for the promise, though it seems far off to others, we do, by faith, realize and embrace, and in it we find a heaven below. Abiding with God and with His people, we consider our situation far better than that of the greatest and most honored of the children of this world. The prospect of our Lord's second coming and of our own eternal glory in fellowship with Him is sufficient to make us content while we wait for His appearing.

This difference on earth will lead to a sad division in death. The child of the bondwoman must be cast out in eternity as well as in time. None can enter heaven who claim that they have earned the right to be there by their own doings, or who boast that they have won it by their own strength. Glory is reserved for those who are saved by grace, and none who trust in self can enter there. What a terrible thing it will be when those who labored to establish their own righteousness, who trusted in their religion and would not submit to the righteousness of Christ, will be driven out! How they will then envy those lowly ones who were pleased to accept pardon through the blood of Jesus! How they will discover their foolishness and wickedness in having despised the gift of God by preferring their own righteousness and religion to that of the Son of God!

> Glory is reserved for those who are saved by grace, and none who trust in self can enter there.

As the people who are represented by Ishmael and Isaac are ultimately parted, so the principles upon which they rest must never be mingled, for they can by no means be made to agree. We cannot be saved partly by self and partly by the promise of God. The principle and notion of earning salvation must be expelled from the mind. Every degree and form of it must be cast out.

If we are so unwise as to place our dependence partly on grace and partly on merit, we will be resting one foot on a rock and the other on the sea, and our fall will be certain. There can be no dividing of the work or of the glory of salvation. It must be all of grace or all of works, all of God or all of man; but it cannot be half of one and half of the other. *And if by grace, then is it not by works; otherwise, the grace is no longer grace. But if it is of works, then it is no longer grace; otherwise, the work is no longer work* (Romans 11:6).

Stop the useless attempt to unite two principles which are as adverse as fire and water. *The promise*, and *the promise* alone, must be the foundation of our hope, and all notions about the law and works and religion must be sternly dismissed as irreconcilable with salvation by grace. We must not begin in the spirit and hope to be made perfect in the flesh (Galatians 3:3). Our Christianity must all be made of one piece. To sow with mingled seed or to wear a garment of linen and woolen mixed was forbidden to the Lord's ancient people, and it is unlawful and useless for us to mix mercy and merit, grace and works. Whenever the notion of salvation by merit, or feeling, or ceremonies comes in, we must cast it out without delay, even though it is as dear to us as Ishmael was to Abraham. Faith is not sight. The spirit is not the flesh. Grace is not merit. We must never forget the distinction, lest we fall into grievous error and miss the heritage that belongs only to the heirs according to promise.

Here is our confession of faith:

> *Knowing that a man is not justified by the*
> *works of the law, but by the faith of Jesus*
> *Christ, even we have believed in Jesus*

> *Christ, that we might be justified by the*
> *faith of Christ, and not by the works of the*
> *law; for by the works of the law shall no*
> *flesh be justified.* (Galatians 2:16)

Here also is the clear line of distinction as to the method of our salvation, and we desire to keep it plain and evident:

> *Even so then at this present time also, there*
> *is a remnant by the gracious election of*
> *God. And if by grace, then is it not by works;*
> *otherwise, the grace is no longer grace. But*
> *if it is of works, then it is no longer grace;*
> *otherwise, the work is no longer work.*
> (Romans 11:5-6)

Do you see this and understand?

Chapter 7

Whose Are the Promises?

Every good gift and every perfect gift is from above and comes down from the Father of lights, with whom is no variableness neither shadow of turning. (James 1:17)

The Lord is always just and good toward His creatures; it is His nature to be so. But there was no necessity either in His justice or in His goodness for Him to make promises of grace to those who had rebelled against Him. Man has forfeited every form of claim upon his Maker which he may have thought he had. He has broken the pure and holy law which he was obligated to have obeyed. God owes nothing to man but the reward of his sins. If God would deal now with man based upon strict justice, He must condemn and punish him. Anything in the way of favor to a guilty creature must proceed only from the undeserved mercy and sovereign goodness of God. It must spring spontaneously from the goodwill and pleasure of the Most High.

The promises of grace flow from the boundless love of God, and from that alone. They could not have proceeded from any other source. No single person in all of mankind has any natural right to promises of blessing, nor can the whole world together deserve them. God has made promises to us of His own free will and good pleasure from no other motive but the love that lies within Himself.

He has chosen to make His promises to His elect, who in the process of time are found out by their exercising faith in Him. Those whom God has chosen are led by the Holy Spirit to choose God and His way of salvation by faith in Christ Jesus. Those of the elect who come to years of circumspection are led to faith in Jesus. All who have faith in Him may conclude beyond doubt that they are of the chosen number to whom the promises are given.

To those who live and die in unbelief, there is no absolute and personal promise of God; they are not under grace, but under law, and to them belong the threatenings and not the promises. These people prefer another method of dealing with God rather than that of gracious promises, and in the end, they perish as the result of their foolish preference. The chosen of the Lord are led to relinquish the proud way of self and merit; they take to the road of faith and so find rest unto their souls. To believe the Word of God and to trust in Him whom God has sent to be our Savior may seem like a small thing, but indeed it is not so. It is the sign of election, the token of regeneration, and the mark of coming glory. To believe that God is true and to rest one's eternal interests upon His promises demonstrates a heart that is reconciled to God and a spirit in which the beginning of perfect holiness is present.

When we believe God as He is revealed in Christ Jesus, we believe all His promises. Confidence in the Person involves confidence in all that He speaks, and so we accept all the promises of God as being sure and certain. We do not trust one promise and doubt another, but we rely upon each one as true, and we believe it to be true to us so far as it is with respect to our condition and circumstances. We argue from general statements to specific applications. He who has said that He will save those who believe in Him will save me, since I believe in Him. Every blessing which He has made available to bestow upon believers, He will bestow upon me as a believer. This is sound reasoning, and by it we justify the faith by which we live and are comforted. I will not receive it because I deserve anything, but because God has freely promised it to me in Christ Jesus; this is the reason and foundation of our hope.

> Yet, so false is the heart of man, that man doubts his Maker.

One wonders at first glance why all people do not believe God. It would seem as if this mark of divine election would be universally present, for God cannot lie, and there is no reason to suspect Him of change or of the lack of ability to keep His word. Yet, so false is the heart of man, that man doubts his Maker. He hates his God, and therefore does not believe Him. It is the surest proof of man's natural enmity against God that he dares to impute falsehood to one who is truth itself. *He that does not believe God has made God a liar; because he does not believe the witness that God has testified of his Son* (1 John 5:10).

Real, practical trust in the living God, easy as it seems to be, is a virtue that was never practiced by an unrenewed heart. The glorious atonement made by the incarnate Son of God is worthy of the trust of all mankind. One would have imagined that every sinner would have washed at once in this cleansing fountain, and without hesitation would have believed in the divine Redeemer; but it is very far from being so. People will not come to Christ in order that they may have life (John 5:40). They would rather trust in anything than in the sacrifice of Jesus. Until the Holy Spirit works a miracle upon a person, that person will not trust in the great sacrifice which God has provided and accepted for the putting away of guilt.

So it is that this simple, commonplace matter of faith becomes the distinguishing mark of the chosen of the Lord. No other mark is so infallible: *He that believes in the Son has eternal life* (John 3:36). Feelings and actions may all serve as evidences, but the master evidence of a claim in the promise of God is faith in Him. *Abraham believed God, and it was counted unto him for righteousness* (Romans 4:3). There were many other good points in the patriarch's character, but this was the decisive one – he believed God. Indeed, this was the root of everything else that was commendable in him.

Worldly-wise men despise faith and set it in contrast with virtuous action, but this contrast is not fair. One might as well contrast a fountain with its stream or the sun with its own heat. If true faith is the mother of holiness, let the mother of grace have praise because of its offspring, and let it not be contrasted therewith. Such

> God loves faith because it honors Him, and also because it leads to acts of obedience to Him.

unfair reasoning comes because of willful malice. If people loved good works as much as they pretend to, they would love the faith which produces them.

God loves faith because it honors Him, and also because it leads to acts of obedience to Him, which includes love for our fellow men. There is more in faith than meets the eye. It is in one aspect the greatest of all good works, even as our Lord Jesus teaches us. The Jews asked Him, *What shall we do that we might work the works of God?* (John 6:28). They would gladly have done godlike works, which the Lord approved above all others. *Jesus answered and said unto them, This is the work of God, that ye believe in him whom he has sent* (John 6:29). This is to say that the most divinely approved work possible is to believe in the Messiah. To trust in the Lord Jesus is the climax of virtue. Proud men may sneer, but this statement is true: *without faith it is impossible to please God* (Hebrews 11:6), but *He that believes on him is not condemned* (John 3:18). The promise is made to those who believe the promise, and to those it will be fulfilled. Those who embrace the promise are embraced by the promise. Those who accept Christ are accepted in Christ. Those who truly believe are surely saved.

Do you believe your God?

Chapter 8

What God Gives is Given Freely

Whereby are given unto us exceeding great and precious promises. (2 Peter 1:4)

Observe that word *given*. Peter says, *Whereby <u>are given</u> unto us exceeding great and precious promises.* We are indebted for everything to the gift of God. We live upon divine charity. All that we have, we have received as a gift, and all we are to have must come in the same way. *For the wages of sin is death, but the grace of God is eternal life in Christ Jesus our Lord* (Romans 6:23). We are unable to earn anything from God, but God is able to give all things. Salvation must be all a gift, a free gift, an undeserved gift, a spontaneous gift of divine love. The promise of salvation is of the same nature.

It is more blessed to give than to receive (Acts 20:35), and He who is most blest of all, the ever-blessed God, delights to give. It is as much His nature to give as it is the nature of the sun to shine or of a river to flow. How blessed we are in being receivers! This is emphasized greatly when we reflect how necessary it is that we should receive things from God; for the things that we need are such that if we do not obtain them, we are lost now, and we will be lost forever. We are without life, without light, without hope, and without peace, if we are without God. If God does not give to us according to the riches of His grace, then we are worse than naked and poor and miserable; we are utterly and altogether undone. It is not possible that we should deserve such rich gifts. Even if we could deserve anything, these must come to us without money and without price. A promise from God must be a blessing of grace. We cannot demand that God promise us His favor and the priceless blessings which are wrapped up in it.

This teaches us what attitude to have. Those dependent upon God have no reason for pride. He who lives upon gifts should be humble and grateful. We are beggars at the door of mercy. At the beautiful gate of the temple, we sit down every day to ask for alms – not from the worshippers, but from Him whom angels worship. As often as our Lord passes by, we ask and He gives, yet we are not surprised that we receive from His love, for He has promised to bestow great mercies. He taught us to say, *Give us this day our daily bread* (Matthew 6:11), and therefore we are neither ashamed nor afraid to ask all things from Him. Ours is a life of dependence, and we delight to have it so. It is sweet to take all things from the hands of our crucified Lord. Happy is the poverty which leads us to be rich in Christ. We earn nothing, and yet receive everything, exceedingly blest in being hourly partakers of the gift of God. *Whereby are given unto us exceeding great and precious promises* (2 Peter 1:4).

Beloved, this teaching as to the promise being a pure gift should be exceedingly encouraging to all who feel their lost condition and who understand and admit that they are spiritually bankrupt. To such people it is a word of good cheer that everything is freely given to us by God. If God gives to us, then why would He not give to them, as well as to other needy ones? Those of us who rejoice in God

> Come, you who are full of sin, and the pardoning Lord will put away your sin.

have received all things as a free gift. Why would others not receive the same? They say, "There is nothing freer than a gift." Why should you not receive God's mercy and love just as I have done?

To one who is willing to give, poverty on the part of the receiver is a recommendation instead of an obstacle. Come, then, you who are without merit; Christ will be your merit. Come, you who have no righteousness; He will be your righteousness. Come, you who are full of sin, and the pardoning Lord will put away your sin. Come, you who are utterly desolate, and be made rich in Jesus. The trade of a beggar will suit you, and you will prosper in it; for I see you have a severe hunger and an empty wallet. He who cannot dig should not be ashamed to beg (Luke 16:3). A beggar needs no merchandise in hand. Old patched shoes, dirty and worn clothing – this is a suitable uniform for a beggar. Are you not dressed in this fashion spiritually? The poorer the wretch, the more welcome he is at the door of divine charity. The less you have of your own, the more welcome you are to Him who gives freely and without reproach (James 1:5).

> Come, ye sinners, poor and wretched,
>   Weak and wounded, sick and sore;
> Jesus, ready, stands to save you,
>   Full of pity, joined with power.
> He is able, He is able;
>   He is willing; doubt no more.
>
> Come, ye needy, come and welcome,
>   God's free bounty glorify;
> True belief and true repentance,
>   Every grace that brings us nigh,
> Without money, without money,
>   Come to Jesus Christ and buy.
>
> Come, ye weary, heavy laden,
>   Bruised and broken by the fall;
> If you tarry 'til you're better,
>   You will never come at all.
> Not the righteous, not the righteous;
>   Sinners Jesus came to call.
>   – Joseph Hart

Yes, it is all a gift. This is the gospel that we are sent to preach to you: *For God so loved the world that he gave his only begotten Son, that whosoever believes in him should not perish but have eternal life* (John 3:16). *And this is the witness, that God has given eternal life to us, and this life is in his Son* (1 John 5:11). On God's part it is all giving; on our part it is all receiving. The promise is already made, and it is freely made. It will be fulfilled, and it will be freely fulfilled. God does not start out giving and then go on to charge a price. No commission is payable upon receipt of His grace. He does not ask or receive a penny. His love is completely a gift. As a gift, you may accept His promise. He will not degrade Himself by listening to any other terms. He gives it at no cost and will not accept any price that you can pay. It has been paid by His Son.

The word given in the text is a plain invitation to the poorest of the poor. Oh, that they would have courage to avail themselves of it! The great bell is ringing. It is ringing so that all who would like to come to the great table of infinite liberality may hear it and draw near. Freely, according to the riches of His grace, God promises salvation and eternal life to all who believe on His Son, Jesus Christ. His promise is firm and sure. Why is it that most do not believe it?

What do you say to the promise so freely given to all believers? Will you believe it and live according to it?

Chapter 9

The Promise of God Is a Reality

Therefore he is able also to save to the uttermost those that come unto God by him, seeing he ever lives to make intercession for them. (Hebrews 7:25)

Surely it is a wonderful thing that the eternal God would make promises to His own creatures. Before He pledged His word, He was free to do as He pleased; but after He has made a promise, His truth and honor bind Him to do as He has said. To Him, indeed, this is no limiting of His liberty, for the promise is always the declaration of His sovereign will and good pleasure. He always delights to act according to His word. Though God is free to do as He pleases, He stoops down to make covenants with us. He does not have to, yet He chooses to do so. The Lord has made a covenant of grace with us in which He has confirmed His promises, not only by pledging His word, but also by giving His oath. *That by two immutable things, in which it is impossible for God to lie, we might have a strong consolation, who have fled for refuge to lay hold upon the hope set before us* (Hebrews 6:18).

In that covenant there are many precious promises, all confirmed in Christ Jesus and established forever upon the foundation of divine truthfulness. This is our hope, even as Paul wrote to Titus: *for the hope of eternal life, which God, who cannot lie, promised before the times of the ages* (Titus 1:2).

God has promised, and on the faithfulness of that promise we build our confidence for time and for eternity. We do not think it is unwise to rest our soul's salvation upon the promise of our faithful Creator. To help us to trust, the promises were not only spoken, but also written. People say they like to have an agreement in black and white, and we have it so in this case. *In the volume of the book it is written of me* (Psalm 40:7; Hebrews 10:7). In the page of inspiration, the testament stands. As we believe our Bibles, we are bound to rely upon the promises contained therein.

It is a cause of much weakness to many that they do not treat the promises of God as realities. If a friend makes them a promise, they regard it as a substantial thing and expect the promise to be kept; but the declarations of God are often viewed as simply words which do not mean much. This is most dishonoring to the Lord, and it is very harmful to ourselves. Rest assured that the Lord never trifles with words: *he said and shall he not do it?* (Numbers 23:19).

His commitments are always kept. David said of the Lord's promises to him: *For he has made an everlasting covenant with me, ordered in all things, and it shall be kept* (2 Samuel 23:5). God speaks deliberately, in due order and determination, and we may depend upon it that His words are sure and will be fulfilled as certainly as they are uttered. Have any who have trusted in the Lord been confounded? Can an instance be found in which our God has been false to His word? The ages cannot produce a single proof that the promise-making God of Israel has run back from that which He has spoken.

Have any who have trusted in the Lord been confounded?

We admire fidelity in men, and we cannot imagine it to be absent from the character of God. Therefore, we may safely count upon His being as good as His word. It is said of Gebhard Leberecht von Blücher that when he was marching to help the Duke of Wellington battle Napoleon at Waterloo, his troops faltered. "It can't be done," they said. "It must be done," was his answer. "I have promised to be there – *promised*, do you hear? You would not have me break my word."

He was at Waterloo according to his word; he would not be hindered, for his promise was given. We praise such faithfulness. We would not think much of one who did not keep his word. Will the Lord God Almighty fail in His promise? No, He will move heaven and earth and shake the universe rather than not fulfill His word. He seems to say, "It must be done. I have promised – promised, do you hear?" In order to keep His promise to us, He spared not His own Son. He considered it better that Jesus die than the word of the Lord be broken. I say again, depend upon it! The Lord means what He says, and He will make good every syllable of His word. Sadly, though, none but the chosen seed will believe Him. Will you believe Him?

No matter who else will lie and deceive, God will be true. If all the truth in the whole world could be gathered together, it would be but as a drop in the bucket compared with the truthfulness of God. The truthfulness of the most honest of men is emptiness itself compared with the sure truth of God. The faithfulness of the most upright of men is as smoke, but the faithfulness of God is as a rock. If we trust in good men, we ought infinitely more to trust in the good God.

Why does it seem to be an unusual thing to rest on the promise of God? Somehow it looks to many to be a dreamy, sentimental, mystical business; and yet if we view it calmly, it is the most matter-of-fact transaction that can be. God is real; all else is unclear. He is certain; all else is questionable. It is an absolute necessity for God to keep His word. How else could He be God? To believe God should be an act of the mind which needs no effort. Even if difficulties could be suggested, the simple and pure in heart should spontaneously say, *For God is true, and every man a liar* (Romans 3:4). To give God less than a wholehearted faith is to rob Him of an honor justly due to His spotless holiness.

Our duty to God demands that we accept His promise and act upon it. Every honest person has a right to be believed, and much more does the God of truth deserve it. We ought to treat the promise as the substance of the actual thing promised, just as we look upon someone's check or promissory note as an actual payment. Promises to pay are passed from hand to hand in daily business as if they were current money of the business owner, and God's promises should be regarded in the same light. Let us believe that we have the petitions which we have asked of Him. He is worthy of our doing so, and He promises to reward such faith.

Let us regard the promise as a thing so sure and certain that we act upon it and make it to be a main figure in all our calculations. The Lord promises eternal life to those who believe in Jesus. Therefore, if we really believe in Jesus, let us conclude that we have eternal life, and let us rejoice in the great privilege. The promise of God is our best ground of assurance; it is far more certain than dreams and visions and fanciful revelations. God's promise is far more to be trusted than feelings, either of joy or sorrow. It is written, *He that believes on him is not condemned* (John 3:18). I believe in Jesus; therefore, I am not condemned. This is good reasoning, and the conclusion is certain. If God has said so, it is so, beyond all doubt. Nothing can be more certain than that which is declared by God Himself. Nothing is more certain to happen than that which He has guaranteed by His own hand and seal.

When a soul is under conviction, it perceives the threatenings of the Lord with an intensity of belief which

> God's promise is far more to be trusted than feelings, either of joy or sorrow.

is very noticeable, since its awe-stricken faith breeds within the heart overwhelming terror and dismay. Why should not the promises be accepted with a similar awareness? Why should they not be accepted with the same certainty? If it is understood in the conscience that *he that believes not shall be condemned*, then it should be accepted with equal assurance that *he that believes and is baptized shall be saved* (Mark 16:16), since the latter is as much the word of God as the former. The tendency of the awakened mind is to dwell upon the dark side of God's Word and to feel the full force of it, while at the same time neglecting the brighter portion of the record and casting doubt upon it, as though it were too good to be true. This is foolish. Every blessing is too good for us to receive if we measure it by our unworthiness, but no blessing is too good for God to give if we judge things by His surpassing excellence. It is after the nature of a God of love to give boundless blessing. If Alexander the Great gave like a king, shall not Yahweh give like a God?

We have sometimes heard people say, "As sure as death." We might as rightly say, "As sure as life." Gracious things from God are as certain as His judgment in righteousness. Whosoever believes in Jesus shall not perish, but has everlasting life (see John 3:16). It must be so, for God's Word has said it, and there can be no mistake about it.

Yes, the Lord means what He says. He never mocks men with barren words and empty sounds. Why would He deceive His creatures and ask from them a worthless trust? The Lord may go beyond His word by giving more than it might be thought to mean, but He can never fall short of it. We may interpret His promises upon the most bountiful scale. He never falls below the largest supply which expectation can give to the promise. Faith never yet outstripped the bounty of the Lord. Let us embrace the promise and rejoice that it is substance and not shadow. Let us even now rejoice in it as being the reality of that for which we are hoping.

Chapter 10

The Special Treasure
of Believers

*But my God shall supply all your need accord-
ing to his riches in glory by Christ Jesus.*
(Philippians 4:19)

God's promises are the special treasure of believers. The substance of faith's heritage lies in
them. All the promises of our covenant God are ours
to have and to hold as our personal possession. By
faith we receive and embrace them, and they consti-
tute our true riches. We enjoy certain precious things
at this present time, but the main part of our wealth,
the bulk of our estate, lies in the promise of our God.
That which we have in hand is only the earnest penny
of the immeasurable wage of grace which is to be paid
to us in due time.

The Lord graciously gives us even now all things
necessary for this life and godliness, but His finest

blessings are held in reserve for time to come. Grace given to us from day to day is our spending money for traveling expenses on the road home, but it is not our fortune. Providential supplies are merely rations on the march, but they are not the ultimate feast of love. We may miss these wayside meals, but we are bound for the *marriage supper of the Lamb* (Revelation 19:9). Thieves may rob us of our ready cash, but our special treasure is hidden with Christ in God beyond all fear of loss. The hand which bled to make this treasure ours is keeping it for us.

> Providential supplies are merely rations on the march, but they are not the ultimate feast of love.

It is a great joy to have a full assurance of our claim in the promises. We may lose this joyful feeling and we may find it hard to get again, yet the eternal inheritance will still be just as certainly ours. It is as though a man would have a copy of his title deed in his hand and would delight himself by reading it, until by some misfortune his copy is stolen or misplaced. The loss of his title deed is not the loss of his rights. He may not be able to read his copy until it is replaced, but his claim to his property is not shaken.

The covenant promise is attached to every joint-heir with Christ, and there is no such thing as the breaking of this attachment. Many events may tend to shake the believer's sense of security, but the promise is *sure to all the seed* (Romans 4:16). Our greatest possession does not lie in any present comfort or confidence which we receive from the promise, but in the promise itself and in the glorious heritage which it secures for us. Our inheritance lies not on this side of Jordan. Our city of habitation is not within the borders of the present life; we see it from afar, but we wait for its full enjoyment in that glorious day when our covenant Head shall be revealed in His glory, and all His people with Him. God's providence is our earthly pension, but God's promise is our heavenly heritage.

Did it ever occur to you to inquire why God deals with His chosen by promises? He could have bestowed His blessings at once and without giving us notice of His intention. In this way, He would have eliminated the necessity of a covenant concerning them. There was no necessity in the nature of things for this plan of promising. The Lord could have given us all the mercies we needed without promising to do so. God, with His great strength of will and firmness of purpose, could have secretly resolved in Himself to do all that He does for believers without having made them the confidants of His divine counsels. He has kept many decrees secret from the time when the foundations of the world were laid; why, then, has He revealed His purposes of blessing? Why is it that His dealings with His people from the gate of Eden until now have been upon the terms of publicly expressed promises?

Does not the question answer itself? In the first place, we could not have been believers if there had not been a promise in which to believe. If the system of salvation is to be by faith, a promise must be made upon which faith can exercise itself. The plan of salvation by faith is selected because it is most suitable to the principle of grace, and this involves the giving of promises, that faith may have both food and foundation. Faith without a promise would be like a foot without ground to stand upon; and such a faith, if it could be called faith, would be unworthy of the plan of grace. With faith being chosen as the great evangelical directive, the promise becomes an essential part of the gospel dispensation.

Moreover, it is a pleasant thought that our good God designedly gives us promises of good things that we may enjoy them twice: first by faith, and then by fruition. He gives twice in giving by promise, and we also receive twice in embracing the promise by faith. The time for the fulfillment of many promises is not in time to come; but by faith we realize the promise, and the foreshadowing of the expected blessing fills our souls with the benefit long before it actually comes.

We have an example of this on a large scale in Old Testament saints. The great promise of the descendants in whom the nations would be blessed was the basis of faith, the foundation of hope, and the cause of salvation to thousands of believers before the Son of God actually appeared among men. Our Lord said, *Abraham rejoiced to see my day, and he saw it and was glad* (John 8:56). The great father of the faithful saw the day of Christ through the telescope of God's promise, by the eye of faith; and though Abraham did not obtain the fulfillment of that promise, but died before the coming of the Lord, as Isaac, Jacob, and many others of the saints did, yet he had Christ to trust in, Christ to rejoice in, and Christ to love and serve. Before He was born in

Bethlehem or offered up on Calvary, Jesus was so seen by the faithful as to make them glad. The promise gave them a Savior before the Savior actually appeared.

So it is with us at this time. By means of the promise, we enter into possession of things not as yet seen. By anticipation, we make the coming blessing present to us. Faith eradicates time, annihilates distance, and brings future things at once into its possession. The Lord has not as yet allowed us to join the hallelujahs of heaven. We have not yet passed through the gates of pearl, nor have we trodden the street of transparent gold; but the promise of such delight lights up the gloom of our affliction and yields us immediate foretastes of glory.

We triumph by faith before our hands actually grasp the palm of victory. We reign with Christ by faith before our heads are encircled with our unfading crowns. Many, many times we have seen the dawn of heaven while we have beheld light breaking from the promise. When faith has been vigorous, we have climbed where Moses stood and gazed upon the land that flows with milk and honey; and then, when Atheist has declared that there is no Celestial City, we have answered, "Did we not see it from the Delectable Mountains?"[3] We have seen enough by means of the promise to make us quite sure of the glory which the Lord has prepared for those who love Him (1 Corinthians 2:9). Thus, we have obtained our first taste of the promised bliss and found therein a sure pledge of our full and final enjoyment of it.

---

3   This is a reference from John Bunyan's allegory, *The Pilgrim's Progress*, which is available from Aneko Press.

Do you not think that the promise is also intended to lead us constantly away from the things that are seen, and onward and upward to the spiritual and the unseen? The one who lives on the promise of God has risen into quite another atmosphere than that which oppresses us in these low-lying valleys of daily life. *It is better to wait upon the LORD than to wait upon man. It is better to trust in the LORD than to put confidence in princes* (Psalm 118:8-9). And so, indeed, it is; for it is more spiritual, more noble, and more inspiring. We need to be raised to this elevated trust by divine power, for our soul naturally cleaves unto the dust.

> Oh, it is a blessed thing for a child of God to be made to exchange the sand of temporal things for the rock of things eternal.

Alas! We are held back by our idolatrous desire to see and touch and handle (see Colossians 2:21). We trust our senses, but we do not have enough sense to trust our God. The same spirit which led Israel to cry in the wilderness, *Make us gods which shall go before us* (Exodus 32:1), leads us to wish for something tangible by flesh and blood upon which our confidence may take hold. We hunger for proofs, tokens, and evidences, and we will not accept the divine promise as better and more certain than all visible signs. So we waste away in hungering for tokens and evidences which are visible, until we are driven to try the better and more certain things which are invisible. Oh, it is a blessed thing for a child of God to be made to exchange the sand of temporal things for the rock of things eternal, by being called upon to walk by the rule of the promise!

Furthermore, the promises are a help to our hearts to know the reality of the Lord Himself. The child of God, when he believes the promise, is brought to feel that God is, and that He is the rewarder of those who diligently seek Him (Hebrews 11:6). Our tendency is to get away from a real God. We live and move in the region of materialism, and we are apt to be captivated by its influences. We feel that our bodies are real when we have pain in them, and we feel this world to be real when we are weighted down with its trouble and difficulties; yet the body is a poor covering, and the world is a mere bubble. Neither will last long. These visible things are insubstantial, but they appear sadly solid to us. What we need is to know that the invisible is just as real as that which is seen, and even more so. We need a living God in this dying world, and we must have Him truly near us, or we will fail. The Lord is training His people to comprehend Himself. The promise is part of this educational process.

When the Lord gives us faith and we rest on His promise, then we are brought face-to-face with Him. We ask, "Who gave this promise? Who is to fulfill this promise?" and our thoughts are thus led into the presence of the glorious God. We feel how necessary He is to the whole system of our spiritual life and how truly He enters into it, so that *in him we live and move and have our being* (Acts 17:28). If the promise cheers us, it is only because God is behind it, for the mere words of the promise are nothing to us except as they come from the lips of God who cannot lie, and except as they are carried out by that hand which cannot fail. The promise is the forecast of the divine purpose and the shadow of the coming blessing. In fact, it is the token of God's own nearness to us.

We must depend upon God for the fulfillment of His word, and that is one of His reasons for dealing with us after the method of promise. Perhaps if the Lord would drop our mercies at our door without a previous hint of their coming, we would not care to know where they came from. If He sends them with unbroken regularity, even as He makes His sun to rise every morning, we might minimalize them as common results of natural laws, and we might forget to depend upon Him because of the punctuality of His providence. Certainly we would lack that grand test of the being and lovingkindness of God which we now receive as we read the promise, accept it by faith, plead it in prayer, and see it fulfilled in due season.

That regularity of divine bounty which ought to sustain and increase faith is often the means of weakening it. He whose bread comes to him by a government annuity or a monthly rent is tempted to forget that God has any hand in it. It shouldn't be this way, but through the hardness of our hearts, such an unfortunate result does frequently follow from the consistency of a gracious providence.

I would not be surprised if those Israelites who were born in the wilderness and had gathered manna every morning for years had also ceased to wonder at it or to see the hand of the Lord in it. Shameful stupidity, but it is quite common! Many people have lived from hand to mouth and have seen the hand of the Lord in the gift of every morsel of bread. In time, by God's goodness, they have prospered in this world and obtained a regular income which they have received without care and trouble, and soon they see it as the natural result of their own hard work, and they no longer praise the lovingkindness of the Lord. To live without the conscious presence of the Lord is a horrible state of affairs. Supplied, but not by God! Sustained, but without the hand of God!

It is better to be poor or sick or exiled, and thus to be driven by our circumstances to approach our heavenly Father. To avoid our coming under the curse of forgetting God, the Lord is pleased to put His choicest blessings into connection with His own promises, and to call forth our faith in reference to them. He will not allow His mercies to become veils to hide His face from the eyes of our love, but He makes them windows through which He looks upon us. The Promiser is seen in the promise, and we watch to see His hand in the performance; in this way, we are saved from that natural atheism which lurks within the heart of man.

I think it is good to repeat that we are put under the system of promise in order that we may grow in faith. How could there be faith without a promise? How could faith grow without grasping more and more of the promise? In the hour of need, we are made to remember that God has said, *Call upon me in the day of trouble: I will deliver thee* (Psalm 50:15). Faith believes this word, calls upon God, and finds itself delivered; thus, it is strengthened and made to glorify the Lord.

Sometimes faith does not find the promise fulfilled right at that moment, but it has to wait awhile. This is fine exercise for it, and serves to test its sincerity and force. This test brings assurance to the believer and fills him with comfort. After a while the answer is given to prayer, the promised blessing is bestowed, faith is crowned with victory, and glory is given to God; but meanwhile, the delay has produced the patience of hope and has made every mercy to wear a double value. Promises provide a training ground for faith. They help us to exercise our young faith so that it can grow to be so strong that it can break through a troop or leap over a wall (2 Samuel 22:30). When our confidence in God is firm, we laugh at impossibility and call out, "It shall be done." This could not happen, though, if there were not an infallible promise with which faith could surround itself.

Those promises which as yet are unfulfilled are precious helps to our advance in the spiritual life. We are encouraged to aspire to higher things by *exceeding great and precious promises.* The prospect of good things to come strengthens us to endure and to press forward. You and I are like little children who are learning to walk and are encouraged to take step after step by an apple being held out to them. We are persuaded to test the trembling legs of our faith by the sight of a promise. Thus, we are drawn to go a step nearer to our God. The little one is very apt to cling to a chair and venture upon its feet, as it is hard to get him to let go of everything; but at last he becomes daring enough for a tiny trip, which ends at his mother's knees. This little venture leads to another and another, until he can run all by himself. The apple plays a great part in the training of the child, and the promise helps us in the education of faith. We have received promise after promise until, I hope, we can give up crawling on the earth and clinging to the things which rest upon it, and we can commit ourselves to the walk of faith.

The promise is a needful implement in the education of our souls in all manner of spiritual graces and actions. I have often said, "My Lord, I have received much from You. Blessed be Your name for it, but there is still one promise more which I have not enjoyed, and therefore I will go forward until I attain its fulfillment! The future is an unknown country, but I enter it with Your promise, and I expect to find in it the same goodness and mercy which have followed me up until now. Yes, I look for greater things than these."

> A promise is, so to speak, the raw material of prayer.

I must not forget to remind you that the promise is part of the management of our spiritual condition here below, because it stirs up prayer. What is prayer but the promise pleaded? A promise is, so to speak, the raw material of prayer. Prayer irrigates the fields of life with the waters which are stored up in the reservoirs of promise. The promise is the power of prayer. We go to God and we say to Him, "Do as You have said. O Lord, here is Your Word; we ask You to fulfill it."

Thus, the promise is the bow by which we shoot the arrows of supplication. In my time of trouble, I like to find a promise which exactly fits my need. Then, I put my finger on it and say, "Lord, this is Your Word; I ask You to prove that it is so by carrying it out in my case. I believe that this is Your own writing, and I ask You to make it good to my faith."

I believe in plenary inspiration,[4] and I humbly look to the Lord for a complete fulfillment of every sentence that He has put on record. I delight to hold the Lord to the very words that He has used, and I expect Him to do as He has said, because He has said it. It is a great thing to be driven to prayer by necessity, but it is a better thing to be drawn to it by the expectation which the promise inspires. Would we pray at all if God did not give us a reason to pray, and then encourage us with gracious promises of an answer? As it is, we are tested in the design of providence, and then we test the promises. We are brought to spiritual hunger, and then we are fed on the *word that proceeds out of the mouth of God* (Matthew 4:4).

By the system which the Lord follows with His chosen, we are kept in constant communion with Him, and we cannot forget our heavenly Father. We are often at the throne of grace, blessing God for promises fulfilled and pleading promises on which we rely. We pay innumerable visits to the divine dwelling place, because we have a promise to plead and a God waiting to be gracious. Is not this a system of things for

---

4   Plenary inspiration means that every word in the Bible is given to us by God and is inspired by God.

which we should be grateful? Should we not magnify the Lord that not only does He pour upon us showers of unpromised blessings, but He also enhances the value of His benefits by making them the subjects of His promises and the objects of our faith?

Chapter 11

The Valuation of
the Promises

*Whereby are given unto us exceeding great
and precious promises.* (2 Peter 1:4)

We have thought upon the promises as our treasure. It is time that we should take a survey of them and calculate their value. Since the promises are our riches, let us form a correct estimate of our wealth. It is possible that we may not fully know how rich we are. It would be a pity to waste away in poverty simply because we are ignorant of our great resources. May the Holy Spirit help us to form a proper valuation of the riches of grace and glory reserved for us in the covenant of promise!

The apostle Peter speaks of the promises as *exceeding great and precious*. They do indeed exceed all things with which they can be compared. No one has ever promised as God has done. Kings have promised even up to half of their kingdoms, but what is that? God promised to give His own Son, and even His own self, to His people, and He did it. Princes draw a line somewhere, but the Lord sets no bounds to the gifts which He ordains for His chosen.

The promises of God not only exceed all precedent, but they also exceed all imitation. Even with God Himself for an example, no one has been able to compete with Him in the language of liberality. The promises of God are as much above all other promises as the heavens are above the earth.

They also exceed all expectation. He does for us *exceeding abundantly above all that we ask or think* (Ephesians 3:20). Nobody could have imagined that the Lord would have made such promises as He has made. They surpass all that we could dream. Even the most cheerful hopes are left far behind, and the loftiest ideas are outdone. The Bible must be true, for it could not have been invented by man. The promises contained in it are greater for quantity and better for quality than the most hopeful person could have looked for. God surprises us with the surpassing fullness of His cheering words. He overwhelms us with blessings until, like Mary, we sit down in wonder and cry, *whence is this to me?* (Luke 1:43).

The promises exceed all measurement: there is a chasm of depth in them as to meaning, a heaven of height in them as to excellence, and an ocean of breadth in them as to duration. We might say of every promise, "It is high; I cannot attain to it." As a whole, the promises exhibit the fullness and all-sufficiency of

God; like God Himself, they fill all things. Unbounded in their range, they are everywhere about us, whether we wake or sleep, whether we go out or return. They cover the whole of life from the cradle to the tomb. A sort of omnipresence may be ascribed to them, for they surround us in all places and at all times. They are our pillow when we fall asleep, and when we awake they are still with us. *How precious are thy thoughts unto me, O God! How great is the sum of them!* (Psalm 139:17). They exceed all conception and calculation; we admire them and adore their Giver, but we can never measure them.

The promises even exceed all experience. Those men of God who have known the Lord for fifty or sixty years have never yet extracted the whole of the marrow from His promise. Still it might be said, *the arrows are beyond thee* (1 Samuel 20:22). Things better and deeper yet remain to be searched out in the future. He who dives deepest by experience into the depths of the divine promises is fully aware that there is yet a deeper depth of grace and love unfathomable. The promise is longer than life, broader than sin, deeper than the grave, and higher than the clouds. He who is most acquainted with the golden Book of promise is still a new beginner in its study. Even the ancients of Israel find that this Book surpasses knowledge.

The promise is longer than life, broader than sin, deeper than the grave, and higher than the clouds.

Certainly, I do not need to say that the promises exceed all expression. If all the tongues of men and of angels were given to me, I would not be able to tell you how great the promises of God are. They exceed not only one language, but all languages. They surpass the glowing praises of all the admirers who have ever spoken. Even angels before the throne still desire to look into these marvels (1 Peter 1:12), for they cannot yet reach the mystery – the length and breadth and height. In Christ Jesus, everything exceeds description. The promises in Him exhaust the force of all speech, human or divine. It is vain for me to attempt the impossible.

Peter says that the promises are *exceeding great*. Peter says they are, and he knew very well. They come from a great God, they assure us of great love, they come to great sinners, they work for us great results, and they deal with great matters. They are as great as greatness itself. They bring us the great God to be our God forever and ever. God's first promise was that in which He committed to give us His Son. We are accustomed to say, *Thanks be unto God for his indescribable gift* (2 Corinthians 9:15), but let not the words glide too easily over the tongue. For God to give His only begotten Son is beyond all conception a great deed of love; indeed, "great" seems too little a word to describe such a miracle of love. When the Lord had given His Son, freely delivering Him up for us all – what then? He promised to give the Holy Spirit, the Comforter, to abide with us forever. Can we measure the value of that great promise? The Holy Spirit came down at Pentecost in fulfillment of that ancient prophecy. Was not that marvelous descent an exceedingly great and precious gift? Remember that the Holy Spirit works in us all those graces which prepare us for the society of heaven. Glory be to God for this visitation of boundless grace!

What next? Our Lord has given us now the promise that He will come again a second time without a sin offering unto salvation (Hebrews 9:28). Can all the saints together fully measure the greatness of the promise of the second coming? This means infinite joy for saints. What else has He promised? He promised that because He lives, we will live also (John 14:19). We will possess an immortality of delight for our souls. We will also enjoy a resurrection of our bodies. We will reign with Christ (2 Timothy 2:12). We will be glorified at His right hand. Promises fulfilled and promises unfulfilled, promises for time and promises for eternity – they are indeed so great that it is impossible to conceive of their being greater.

How firm a foundation, ye saints of the Lord,
　　Is laid for your faith in His excellent Word!
What more can He say than to you He hath said –
　　To you who for refuge to Jesus have fled?[5]

You whose minds are trained to think high thoughts, tell me your estimate of the faithful promises! I find a promise of the pardon of sin. You forgiven ones, declare the greatness of this blessing! There is the promise of adoption (Ephesians 1:5). Children of God, you begin to know what manner of love the Father has granted to you in this; proclaim your joy! There is the promise of *help in time of need* (Hebrews 4:16). You who have

---

5　From the hymn "How Firm a Foundation," author uncertain

been through trials, you know how the Lord sustains and delivers His chosen; proclaim the greatness of His grace! There is the promise that *as thy days, so shall thy strength be* (Deuteronomy 33:25). You who are working hard for Christ or bearing His cross from day to day, you feel how exceedingly great is that promise of sure support. What a wonderful word is this: *he will not withhold good from those that walk uprightly* (Psalm 84:11)! What a sentence this is: *all things work together for good to them that love God, to them who are the called according to his purpose* (Romans 8:28 KJV)!

Who can estimate the breadth of such a gracious assurance? No, you do not need to take that tape measure from your pocket; it will not do you any good here. If you could take the distance of a fixed star as your base, all calculations would still be impossible. All the chains that ever measured the acres of the wealthy are useless here. A certain millionaire glories that his estate reaches from sea to sea, but no ocean can bound the possessions secured to us by the promise of our faithful God. The theme is so exceedingly great that it exceeds my power of expression, and therefore I desist.

The verse upon which we are now thinking speaks of *exceeding great and precious promises.* Greatness and preciousness seldom go together, but in this instance, they are closely united. When the Lord opens His mouth to make a promise, it is sure to be worthy of Him. He speaks words of exceeding power and richness. Instead of trying to speak of the preciousness of the promises doctrinally, I will fall back upon the experience of those who have tried and proved them.

Beloved, how precious the promises are to the poor and needy! Those who realize their spiritual poverty discern the value of the promise which meets their case. How precious also are the promises to those who have enjoyed the fulfillment of them! We can go back in memory to times and seasons when we were brought low and the Lord helped us according to His Word. Even before He brought us up out of the horrible pit, we were kept from sinking in the deep mire by looking forward to the time when He would appear for our rescue. His promise kept us from dying of hunger long before we reached the feast of love. In the expectation of future trial, our confidence is in the promise, and so it is very precious to us even before it is actually fulfilled.

> So precious is the Word of the Lord to us, that we could part with everything we have rather than throw away a single sentence of it.

The more we believe the promise, the more we find in it to believe. So precious is the Word of the Lord to us, that we could part with everything we have rather than throw away a single sentence of it. We cannot tell which promise of the Lord we may need next. That which we have hardly noticed may yet turn out at a certain moment to be essential to our life. Thank God that we are not called to part with any one of the jewels from the breastplate of Holy Scripture. *For all the promises of God are yes in him, and in him Amen, by us for the glory of God* (2 Corinthians 1:20).

How precious are the promises when we lie sick,

gazing into eternity months at a time, sorely tried and tempted through pain and weariness! All depressing circumstances lose their power for evil when our faith takes firm hold upon the promises of God. How sweet to be aware that I have my head and my heart on the promise. I rest on the truth of the Most High! Not on earthly futility, but on heavenly truth do I rest. There is nothing to be found elsewhere comparable to this perfect rest. The pearl of peace is found among the precious promises. That which can support dying men is precious indeed, and can cause them to pass into eternity with as much delight as if they were going to a marriage feast. That which lasts forever, and joyfully lasts forever, is most precious. That which brings all things with it, and has all things in it, that is precious indeed; and such is the promise of God.

If this is the greatness and preciousness of the promises, let us joyfully accept and believe them. Will the child of God believe me? Perhaps, but if not me, certainly he will believe his own Father. Certainly, it ought to be the easiest thing in the world for the sons and daughters of the Most High to believe in Him who has given them power to become the children of God. My brothers and sisters, let us not stagger at the promise through unbelief, but let us fully believe!

Furthermore, let us know the promises. Should we not carry them at our fingertips? Should we not know them better than anything else? The promises should be the classics of believers. Even if you have not read the latest new book and have not heard about the latest vote of the government, you should know very well what the Lord God has said, and you should look to see His word made good. We ought to be so familiar with the Bible as to always have at the tip of our tongue the promise which most exactly meets our case. We ought to be transcripts of Scripture. The divine promise should be as much written upon our hearts as upon the pages of the Book. It is a sad pity that any child of God should be unaware of the existence of the royal promise which would enrich him. It is pitiful for any one of us to be like the poor man who had

> What is the use of having an anchor at home when your ship is in a storm at sea?

a fortune left to him of which he knew nothing, and so he continued sweeping the streets and begging for money. What is the use of having an anchor at home when your ship is in a storm at sea? What good is a promise which you cannot remember so as to plead it in prayer? Whatever else you do not know, try to be familiar with those words of the Lord which are more needful to our souls than bread is to our bodies.

Let us also make use of the promises. A little while ago, a friend gave me a check for certain charities, and he said to me, "Be sure that you deposit it into the bank today." You may rest assured that this was done. I do not keep checks to look at and play with; they go to the bank, and the cash is received and used.

The precious promises of our great God are distinctly intended to be taken to Him and exchanged for the blessings which they guarantee. Prayer takes the promise to the Bank of Faith and obtains the golden blessing. Take care how you pray. Make real business of it. Let it never be a dead formality. Some people pray a long time, but do not get what they are supposed to ask for because they do not plead the promise in a truthful, businesslike way. If you were to go into a bank and stand for an hour talking to the clerk, and then come out again without your cash, what would be the good of it? If I go to a bank, I pass my check across the counter, take my money, and go about my business. That is the best way of praying. Ask for what you need according to His will, because the Lord has promised it. Believe that you have the blessing, and go out to your work in full assurance of it. Get up from your knees singing because the promise is fulfilled. Then your prayer will be answered. It is not the length of your prayer, but the strength of your prayer that wins with God; and the strength of prayer lies in your faith in the promise which you have pleaded before the Lord.

Lastly, talk about the promises. Tell the King's household what the King has said. Never keep God's lamps under bushels. Promises are proclamations. Display them on the wall. Read them aloud at the marketplace. Oh, that our conversations were more often sweetened with the precious promises of God! After dinner, we often sit around for half an hour and complain about our pastors or gossip about our neighbors. How often this is our Sunday's amusement! It would be far better if we said, "Now, friend, quote a promise," and if the other replied, "And you mention a promise too." Then let each one speak according to his own personal knowledge concerning the Lord's fulfillment of those promises, and let everyone present tell the story of the Lord's faithfulness to him. By such holy conversations we would warm our own hearts, gladden one another's spirits, and the Sabbath would thus be rightly spent.

Businessmen speak of their trade, travelers tell of their adventures, and farmers talk about their crops. Should we not, then, abundantly proclaim the Lord's goodness and talk of His faithfulness? If we did so, we would all show our approval of Peter's statement that our God has given unto us *exceeding great and precious promises.*

Chapter 12

God Fulfills His Promises

And the LORD gave Solomon wisdom as he promised him. (1 Kings 5:12)

How the Lord brought about wisdom in Solomon I do not know, but He promised that He would give him wisdom, and He kept His word. The more you think of this, the more remarkable will the fact appear. Solomon was not born under the most hopeful circumstances for wisdom. As the darling child of a somewhat aged father, he was highly likely to be spoiled. As a young man who came to the throne before he was at all ready for it in the course of nature, he was very likely to have made great blunders and mistakes. As a man of strong animal passions, which in the end overpowered him, he seemed more likely to prove to be a degenerate than a philosopher. As a person possessing great wealth, unlimited power, and constant prosperity, he had little of that difficult experience through which people acquire wisdom.

Who were his teachers? Who taught him to be wise? His remorseful mother may have taught him much sound morality and religion, but she could never have imparted to him the eminent degree of wisdom which raised him above all other men and set him upon the pinnacle of renown. He knew more than others, and therefore could not have borrowed his wisdom from them. Wise men sat at his feet, and his fame brought pilgrims from the ends of the earth; none of these could have been his tutors, since he surpassed them all. How did this man rise to absolute preeminence in wisdom so as to make his name throughout all time synonymous for a wise man?

This creation of such a great mind is a very mysterious process. Who will give a young man wisdom? You can impart knowledge to him, but not wisdom. No tutor, master, or religious leader can give another man wisdom. They have to work much to get a little of it for themselves, yet God gave Solomon largeness of heart as the sands of the sea, and wisdom unrivaled; for God can do all things. By means known only to Himself, the Lord produced in the young king a capacity for observation, reasoning, and prudent action that has been seldom, if ever, equaled. We have often admired the wisdom of Solomon. I invite you still more to admire the wisdom of God, by whom Solomon's marvelous genius was produced.

The reason why the Lord worked this wonder upon Solomon was because He had promised to do it, and

He is sure to keep His word. Many other Bible verses would serve my purpose as well as this one, for all I desire to bring out of it is this: that whatever God has promised to anyone, He will surely give it to him. Whether it is wisdom to Solomon or grace to you, if the Lord has made the promise, He will not allow it to go unfulfilled. The God who performed His word in this very remarkable instance regarding Solomon, where the matter was so entirely beyond human power and was surrounded with such disadvantageous

God will always keep His word to the letter, and He will usually go beyond what the letter seems to mean.

circumstances, will accomplish His promise in other cases, however difficult and mysterious the fulfilling of that promise may seem to be. God will always keep His word to the letter, and He will usually go beyond what the letter seems to mean.

In this instance, while He gave Solomon wisdom, He also added to him riches and a thousand other things which did not appear in the promise. *Seek ye first the kingdom of God and his righteousness, and all these things shall be added unto you* (Matthew 6:33). He who makes promises about infinite blessings will throw in everyday things as if they were of small account and were given as a matter of course.

From the case of Solomon and thousands more of a similar kind, we learn first that the foundational point of God's giving is *as He has promised*.

The pages of history sparkle with instances of this. The Lord promised to our fallen parents that the seed of the woman would bruise the serpent's head (Genesis 3:15); behold, that wondrous Seed of the woman has appeared, and has gotten for Himself, and for us, the glorious victory of our redemption! In the fulfillment of that one promise we have security that all the rest of God's promises will be kept. When God promised Noah that he would be safe upon entering the ark, he found it so. Not one of those innumerable waves which destroyed the pre-flood world could break into his place of safety. When God said to Abraham that He would give him descendants and a land which would be the possession of those descendants, it seemed impossible; but Abraham believed God, and in due time he rejoiced to behold Isaac and to see in him the promised heir.

When the Lord promised Jacob that He would be with him and do him good, He kept His word and gave him the deliverance for which he wrestled at the brook Jabbok. That long-delayed answer to the promise, that the descendants of Israel would possess the land which flowed with milk and honey, seemed as if it would never be accomplished. The tribes of Israel were reduced to slavery in Egypt, and Pharaoh held them with an iron grip and would not let them go. But God, who undertook for His people, brought them out with a high hand and with an outstretched arm on the very day in which He promised to rescue them. He divided the Red Sea also, and He led His people through the wilderness, for He had assured them that He would do so. He divided the Jordan River in half, and He drove out the Canaanites before His people, giving to Israel the land for their inheritance, just as He had promised.

The history of the Lord's faithfulness is so voluminous that time would fail us to tell of all the instances. God's words have always in due time been justified by God's acts. God has dealt with people according to His promise. Whenever they have taken hold upon the promise and said, "Do as You have said," God has responded to the plea and proved that it was no vain thing to trust Him. Throughout all time, it has been God's unvarying rule to keep His word to the letter and to the moment.

> The history of the Lord's faithfulness is so voluminous that time would fail us to tell of all the instances.

"This is big talk," someone says. All right, then, we will descend to smaller talk. It is God's way to keep His promise to each individual. We ourselves are living witnesses that God does not forget His word. Tens of thousands of us can testify that we have trusted in Him and have never been let down. I was once a brokenhearted sinner, cowering down beneath the black cloud of almighty wrath, guilty and self-condemned, and I felt that if I were banished forever from God's presence, I could not rightly say one word against the justice of the sentence. When I read in His word, *If we confess our sins, he is faithful and just to forgive us our sins* (1 John 1:9), I went to Him. Tremblingly, I was determined to test His promise. I acknowledged my transgressions unto the Lord, and He forgave the iniquity of my sin. I am telling no empty story, for the deep, restful peace which came to my heart in the moment of forgiveness was such that it seemed as if I had begun a new life – and indeed, I had.

This is how it came about: one Lord's Day I heard a man speak upon that promise, *Look unto me, and be ye saved, all the ends of the earth* (Isaiah 45:22). I could not understand how a simple look to Christ could save me. It seemed too simple an act to bring about so great a result; but, as I was ready to try anything, I looked – I looked to Jesus.

It was all I did. It was all I could do. I looked unto Him who is set forth as a propitiation for sin (1 John 2:2), and in an instant, I knew that I was reconciled to God. I saw that if Jesus suffered in my place, then I could not suffer too. I saw that if He bore all my sin, I had no more sin to bear. My iniquity must be blotted out if Jesus took it in my place and endured all its penalty.

With that thought there came into my spirit a sweet sense of peace with God through Jesus Christ my Lord. The promise was true, and I found it to be so. It happened about thirty-six years ago, but I have never lost the sense of that complete salvation which I then found, nor have I lost that peace which so sweetly dawned upon my spirit. Since then, I have never relied in vain upon a promise of God. I have been placed in positions of great danger, have known great need, have felt sharp pain, and have been weighed down with never-ending concerns; but the Lord has been true to every line of His Word, and when I have trusted Him, He has carried me through everything without a failure. I am constrained to speak well of Him, and I do so. To this, I set my hand and seal, without hesitation or reserve.

The experience of all believers is much the same. We began our new lives of joy and peace by believing the promise-making God, and we continue to live in the same manner. A long list of fulfilled promises is present to our happy memories, awakening our gratitude and confirming our confidence. We have tested the faithfulness of our God year after year in a great many ways, but always with the same result. We have gone to Him with promises of the common things of life relating to daily bread and clothing and children and home, and the Lord has dealt graciously with us. We have turned to Him concerning sickness and slander and doubt and temptation, and He has never failed us. In little things, He has been mindful of us. Even the hairs of our head have been numbered. When it appeared very unlikely that the promise could be kept, God fulfilled it with remarkable exactness. We have been broken down by the falseness of man, but we have rejoiced and continue to rejoice in the truthfulness of God. It brings tears to our eyes to think of the startling ways in which Yahweh, our God, has worked to carry out His gracious promises.

> Thus far we prove that promise good,
> Which Jesus ratified with blood:
> Still He is gracious, wise, and just,
> And still in Him let Israel trust.
> – Philip Doddridge

Let me freely speak to all who trust in the Lord. Children of God, has not your heavenly Father been true to you?

Is not this your constant experience, that you are always failing, but He never fails? Well said the apostle Paul, *If we are unfaithful, yet he remains faithful; he cannot deny himself* (2 Timothy 2:13). We may interpret divine language in its broadest sense, and we will find that the Lord's promise is kept to the utmost of its meaning. The rule of His giving is large and generous. The promise is an immense container, and the Lord fills it to overflowing. As the Lord in Solomon's case gave him *as he promised him*, so He will do in every instance as long as the world stands. Believe the promise and prove yourself to be an inheritor of it. May the Holy Spirit lead you to do this, for Jesus's sake!

Chapter 13

The Rule without Exception

Blessed be the LORD that has given rest unto his people Israel according to all that he had said; not one word has failed of all his good word, which he spoke by the hand of Moses, his slave. (1 Kings 8:56)

God gives good things to us according to His promise.

This is a matter of fact and not a mere opinion. We declare it and defy all the world to bring any evidence to disprove the statement.

Upon this point I am a personal witness. My experience has been long and my observation has been wide, but I have never yet met with a person who trusted God and found the Lord's promise to fail him. I have seen many living men sustained under heavy trials by resting in the word of the Lord, and I have also seen many dying people made triumphant in death by the same means; but I have never met with a believer who has been made ashamed of his hope because of his earthly afflictions, nor with one who on his deathbed has repented of trusting in the Lord.

All my observation points the other way and confirms me in the persuasion that the Lord is faithful to all who rely upon Him. I am prepared to testify in a court of law about this if called upon to do so. I would not utter a falsehood under the pretext of a pious fraud, but I would testify upon this important subject as an honest witness without reserve or indecisiveness. I never knew a man in the pangs of death lament that he trusted the Savior. No, and what is more, I have never heard that such a thing has happened anywhere at any time. If there had been such a case, the haters of the gospel would have advertised it high and low. Every street would have heard the evil news. Every preacher would have been confronted with it. We would have been met with pamphlets at the door of every church and chapel, reporting that such a person who had lived a saintly life and who had relied on the Redeemer's merits had discovered in his last hours that he had been deceived and that the doctrine of the cross was all delusion. We challenge opponents to discover such an instance. Let them find it among rich or poor, old or young. Let the very fiend himself, if he can, bear witness to the failure of a single promise of the living God. But it has not been said that Yahweh has deceived one of His people, and it never will be said; for God is true to every word that He has ever spoken.

God never lowers Himself to a lie. The mere idea

of such a thing is blasphemous. Why should He be false? What is there about Him that could cause Him to break His word? It would be contrary to His nature. How could He be God and not be just and true? He cannot, therefore, violate His promise through any lack of faithfulness.

Furthermore, the omnipotent God never promises beyond His power. We frequently intend to act according to our word, but we find ourselves mastered by overwhelming circumstances, and our promise falls to the ground because we are unable to perform it. It can never be so with the almighty God, for His ability is without limit. All things are possible with Him (Matthew 19:26).

> The omnipotent God never promises beyond His power.

Our promise may have been made in error, and we may afterwards discover that it would be wrong to do as we have said; but God is infallible, and therefore His word will never be withdrawn because of a mistake. Infinite wisdom has set its approval upon every promise; each word of the Lord is registered by unerring judgment and ratified by eternal truth.

Neither can the promise fail because of a change in the Divine Promiser. We change – poor, frail things that we are! But the Lord knows *no variableness neither shadow of turning* (James 1:17). Therefore, His word abides forever the same. Because He does not change, His promises stand fast like the great mountains. Has God said it, *and shall he not do it?* (Numbers 23:19).

Our strong comfort rests upon the unchanging ways and character of God.

Nor can the word of the Lord fall to the ground through forgetfulness on His part. Sometimes our tongues outrun our hands; for although we are willing, we sometimes fail to do what we say because other things come in and distract our attention. We might forget or lose interest, but it is never so with the Faithful Promiser. His most ancient promise is still fresh in His mind, and He means it as much now as He did when He first uttered it. He is, in fact, always giving the promise, since there is no time with Him. The old promises of Scripture are new promises to faith, for every word still proceeds out of the mouth of the Lord to be bread for men (Deuteronomy 8:3; Matthew 4:4).

Because of all this, the word of the Lord deserves all faith, both direct and indirect. We can trust men too much, but we can never trust God too much. It is the surest thing that has been or that can ever be. To believe His word is to believe what no one can rightly question. Has God said it? Then it must be so. *The heaven and the earth shall pass away, but my words shall not pass away* (Matthew 24:35). The laws of nature may be suspended: fire may cease to burn and water may cease to drown, for this would involve no unfaithfulness in God; but for His word to fail would involve a dishonoring change in the character and nature of the Godhead, and this can never be. Let us confirm that God is true, and never allow the slightest suspicion of His truthfulness to cross our minds.

The immutable word of promise is, and ever must

be, the foundation of God's giving. Consider a little while, as I make a further observation; namely, that against this, no other rule can stand. No other law, supposed or real, can ever come into conflict with the standard of God's promise.

The law of deserving is sometimes set up against it, but it cannot prevail. "Oh," someone says, "I cannot think that God can or will save me, for there is no good thing in me!" You speak correctly, and your fear cannot be removed if God is to act toward you upon the principle of deserving. But if you believe on His Son, Jesus, that principle will not operate, for the Lord will act toward you according to the principle of His promise. The promise was not founded upon your merits; it was freely made, and it will be just as freely kept. If you inquire how God can meet you even though you do not deserve it, let me remind you of Jesus who came to save you from your sins. The boundless merits of the Lord Jesus are set to your account, and your awful demerits are thereby neutralized once for all. The law of merit would sentence you to destruction as you stand in yourself; but he who believes is not under law but under grace, and under grace the great Lord deals with us according to pure mercy as revealed in His promise. Choose not to be self-righteous, or justice must condemn you. Be willing to accept salvation as a free gift bestowed through the application of the sovereign right of God, who says, *I will have mercy on whom I will have mercy* (Exodus 33:19; Romans 9:15). Be humbly trustful in the grace of God which is revealed in Christ Jesus, and the promise will be richly fulfilled to you.

The Lord does not deal with us according to the measure of our moral ability. "Oh," says the seeker, "I think I might be saved if I could make myself better or become more religious or exercise greater faith, but I am without strength. I cannot believe. I cannot repent. I cannot do anything right!" Remember, then, that the gracious God has not promised to bless you according to the measure of your ability to serve Him, but according to the riches of His grace as declared in His Word. If His gifts were given according to your spiritual strength, you would get nothing, for you can do nothing without the Lord. But, as the promise is kept according to the infiniteness of divine grace, there can be no question about it.

You do not need to stagger at the promise through unbelief, but only consider that He who has promised is able also to accomplish it. Do not limit the Holy One of Israel by imagining that His love is restricted by your ability. The volume of the river is not to be calculated by the dryness of the desert through which it flows; there is no logical proportion between the two. With only half an eye, one can see that there is no calculating the extent of infinite love by measuring human weakness. The operations of almighty grace are not limited by mortal strength or lack of strength. God's power will keep God's promise.

Your weakness cannot defeat God's promise, and your strength cannot fulfill the promise. He who spoke the word will Himself make it good. It is neither your duty nor mine to keep God's promises. That is His obligation and not ours. Poor helpless one, attach your heavy wagon of incapacity to the great engine of the promise, and you will be drawn along the lines of duty and blessing! Though you are more dead than alive, and though you have more weakness than strength, this will not affect the certainty of the divine fulfillment. The power of the promise lies in Him who made the promise. Therefore, look away from self and look to God. If you are weak, rest in the arms of the Divine Promiser. If you consider yourself dead, then be buried in the grave where the bones of a promise lie, and you will be made alive as soon as you touch them (see 2 Kings 13:21).

Look away from self and look to God.

What we can or cannot do is not the question, but everything hinges upon what the Lord can do. It is enough for us to keep our own contracts without attempting to keep God's promises. I would not like my fellow man to question my financial trustworthiness because a beggar who lives on the next street cannot pay his debts. Why, then, should I doubt the Lord because I have profound reasons to distrust myself? My ability is quite another question from the faithfulness of God, and it is a pity to mix the two things. Let us not dishonor our God by dreaming that His arm is not capable simply because our arm has grown weak or weary.

Neither must we measure God by the standard of our feelings. We often hear the excuse that "I do not feel that I can be saved. I do not feel that such sin as mine can be forgiven. I do not feel that it is possible that my hard heart can ever be softened and renewed." This is foolish talk. In what way can our feelings guide us in such matters? Do you feel that the dead in their graves can be raised again? Do you even feel that the cold of winter will be followed by the heat of summer? How can you feel these things? You do not feel them, but you believe them. To talk of feeling in these matters is absurd. Does the fainting man feel that he will revive? Is it not the nature of such a state to suggest death? Do dead bodies feel that they will have a resurrection? Feeling is out of the question.

God gave Solomon wisdom as He had promised him, and He will give you what He has promised, whatever your feelings may be. If you look through the book of Deuteronomy, you will see how often Moses uses the expression *as he has promised*. He says, The Lord *bless you, as he has promised* (Deuteronomy 1:11). He cannot pronounce on Israel a larger benediction. That holy man viewed the dealings of the Lord with constant admiration, because they were *as he has promised*. In our case also, the standard of the Lord's dealings will be *as he has promised*. Our experience of divine grace will not be "as we now feel," but *as he has promised*.

While writing these things for the comfort of others, I find it necessary to confess that personally, my feelings often change, but I have learned to set very small importance on them, either one way or the other. Above all, I have stopped trying to estimate the truth of the promise by the condition of my mind. Today, I feel so joyful that I could dance to the tune of Miriam's timbrel, but perhaps when I wake tomorrow morning

I will only be able to sigh in harmony with Jeremiah's lamentations. Has my salvation changed according to these feelings? If so, then it must have had a very unsure foundation. Feelings are more changing than the winds, more unsubstantial than bubbles. Are these to be the gauge of the divine dependability?

States of mind often depend upon the condition of the liver or the stomach. Are we to judge the Lord by these? Certainly not. The state of the barometer may send our feelings up or down; can there be much dependence upon things so changeable? God does not hang His eternal love upon our emotions. That would be like building a temple on a wave. We are saved according to facts, not according to fancies. Certain eternal truths prove us saved or lost, and those truths are not affected by our euphoria or depressions. Do not set up your feelings as a test by which to determine the truthfulness of the Lord! Such conduct is a sort of mingled insanity and wickedness. If the Lord has said the word, He will make it good, whether you feel triumphant or despondent.

Again, God will not give to us according to the terms of probabilities. It seems very improbable that you, my friend, should be blessed of the Lord who made heaven and earth; but if you trust the Lord, you are favored as surely as the blessed Virgin herself, of whom it is said that all generations shall call her blessed (Luke 1:48). It is written, *blessed is she that believed, for there shall be a performance of those things which were told her from the Lord* (Luke 1:45). *O LORD of the hosts, happy is the man that trusts in thee* (Psalm 84:12).

It may seem improbable that an old sinner, saturated in sin, should at once begin a new life by believing in Jesus, and yet it will be so. It may seem very unlikely that a woman living in sin would hear that word, *He that believes in me has eternal life* (John 6:47), would immediately lay hold upon it, and would at once receive everlasting life; yet it is true, and I have seen it so.

Our God is a God of wonders. Things improbable, even impossible with us, are everyday things with Him. He causes the camel, despite its hump, to go through the needle's eye. He calls the things which are not as though they were. Do you laugh at the very idea of your being saved? Let it not be the distrustful laugh of Sarai, but the joyous expectancy of Abraham. Believe on Jesus, and you will laugh all over, inwardly and outwardly, not from disbelief, but for quite another reason. When we know God, we do not cease to wonder, but we begin to be at home with wonders. Believe the promise of God's grace, and believing, you will live in a new world which will always be a land of wonder to you. It is a happy thing to have such faith in God as to expect as certain that which to mere human judgment is most unlikely. *With God all things are possible* (Matthew 19:26). It is therefore possible that He would save every soul that believes in Jesus. The law of gravity acts in all cases, and so does the law of divine faithfulness.

There are no exceptions to the rule that God will keep His covenant. Extreme cases, difficult cases, even impossible cases, are included within the circle of the

Lord's Word, and therefore no one needs to despair or even doubt. God's opportunity has come when man's extremity is reached. The worse the case, the more certain it is to be helped by the Lord. Oh, that you would do the Lord the honor of believing in Him and leaving all in His hands!

How long will it be before people will trust their God? *O thou of little faith, why didst thou doubt?* (Matthew 14:31). Oh, that we would settle it in our minds that we would never again distrust the Faithful One!

For God is true, and every man a liar (Romans 3:4). The Lord Himself says, *Is the LORD's hand waxed short? Thou shalt see now whether my word shall come to pass unto thee or not.* (Numbers 11:23). Let not the Lord speak this way to us in anger, but let us believe and be sure that the solemn declarations of the Lord must be fulfilled. Speak no longer one to another, asking, "What is truth?" Know infallibly that the Word of the Lord is sure and endures forever.

Here is a promise with which you can begin. Test it and see that it is true: *call upon me in the day of trouble: I will deliver thee, and thou shalt glorify me* (Psalm 50:15).

Chapter 14

Taking Possession of the Promise

I AM the God of Abraham, thy father, and the God of Isaac; the land upon which thou dost lie, to thee will I give it. (Genesis 28:13)

Timid people find much difficulty in laying hold of the promises of God as being made to themselves. They are afraid that it would be presumptuous to grasp things so good and precious. As a general rule, we may consider that if we have faith to grasp a promise, that promise is ours. He who gives us the key that will fit the lock of His door intends for us to open the door and enter. There can never be presumption in humbly believing God; there may be a great deal of it in daring to question His Word. We are not likely to err in trusting the promise too far. Our failure lies in lack of faith and not in too much of it. It would be hard to believe God too much. It is dreadfully common to believe Him too little. *According to your faith be it unto you* (Matthew 9:29) is a benediction from which the Lord will never draw back. *If thou canst believe this, all things are possible to him that believes* (Mark 9:23). It is written, *they could not enter in because of their unbelief* (Hebrews 3:19), but it is never said that one who entered in by faith was admonished for his presumption and driven out again.

Jacob, according to the text with which we have headed this chapter, took possession of the promised land by stretching himself upon it and going to sleep. There is no surer way of taking possession of a promise than by placing your whole weight upon it and then enjoying a good rest. *The land upon which thou dost lie, to thee will I give it.*

> There is no surer way of taking possession of a promise than by placing your whole weight upon it and then enjoying a good rest.

How often have I found the promise true to my own self when I have accepted it as truth and have acted upon it! I have stretched myself upon it as upon a couch, and I left myself in the hands of the Lord; then, a sweet rest covered my spirit. Confidence in God realizes its own desires. The promise which our Lord made to those who seek favors in prayer sounds like this: *believe that ye receive it, and it shall come upon you* (Mark 11:24). This sounds strange, but it is true; it is according to the philosophy of faith. Say, by a realizing faith, "This promise is mine," and immediately it is yours. It is by faith that we receive promises, and not by sight and sense.

The promises of God are not enclosures to be the private property of this Christian or that one, but they are an open common for all the dwellers in the community of holy faith. No doubt there are persons who would, if they could, own the stars and make a personal estate out of the sun and moon. The same greed might put limitations around the promises, but this cannot be done. Misers might as well try to hedge in the songbirds and claim the music of the lark and thrush as their own sole inheritance as propose to keep God's promises all to themselves. No, not the best of the saints can, even if they wished to do so, put a single word of the God of grace under lock and key. The promise is not only *unto you and to your children*, but also *to all that are afar off, even as many as the Lord our God shall call* (Acts 2:39). What a comfort this is! Let us take up our common rights and possess by faith what the Lord has made ours by a covenant of salt.

Words spoken to Jacob belong equally to all believers. Hosea says of him, *Yea, he dominated the angel and prevailed; he wept and made supplication unto him; he found him in Bethel, and there he spoke with us* (Hosea 12:4). So the Lord God spoke with us when He spoke with the patriarch. The wonders which God displayed at the Red Sea were performed for all His people, for we read, *there did we rejoice in him* (Psalm 66:6). It is true that we were not there, and yet the joy of Israel's victory is ours. The apostle quotes the word of the Lord to Joshua as if it were spoken to any and every child of God: *he has said, I will never leave thee, nor forsake thee* (Hebrews 13:5). No word of the Lord ends with the occasion with which it began, or wears itself out in blessing the individual to whom it was first addressed. All the promises are for believers who have faith enough to embrace them and plead them at the throne of grace. What God is to one who trusts Him, He will be to all in a similar way according to their circumstances and necessities.

The Bible has its eye upon each one of us as it utters its words of grace. John Miller, a speaker in 1817 at the annual Bampton lectures at the University of Oxford, has well said, "We, ourselves, and such as we, are the very persons whom Scripture speaks of, and to whom, as men, in every variety of persuasive form, it makes its condescending, though celestial, appeal. The point worthy of observation is, to note how a book of the description and the compass which we have represented Scripture to be, possesses this versatility of power, this eye, like that of a portrait, uniformly fixed upon us, turn where we will."

> Eye of God's word! where'er we turn,
>   Ever upon us! thy keen gaze
> Can all the depths of sin discern,
>   Unravel every bosom's maze.
>
> "What word is this? Whence know'st thou me?"
>   All wondering cries the humbled heart,
> To hear thee that deep mystery,
>   The knowledge of itself, impart.
>   – From "St. Bartholomew," by John Keble

This singular personality of the word to each one of a thousand generations of believers is one of its greatest charms and one of the most certain proofs of its divine inspiration. We do not treat our Bibles as old almanacs, but as books for the present – new, fresh, and adapted for the hour. Abiding sweetness dwells in undiminished freshness in the ancient words upon which our fathers fed in their day. Glory be to God, we are feasting on them still; or if we are not, we ought to be, and we can only blame ourselves if we do not!

> Abiding sweetness dwells in undiminished freshness in the ancient words upon which our fathers fed in their day.

The wells of Abraham served for Isaac and Jacob and a thousand generations. Come, let us let down our buckets, and with joy draw water out of the old wells of salvation, dug in the far-off days when our fathers trusted in the Lord, and He delivered them! We do not need to fear that we shall be naive or too trusting. The promises of the Lord are made to all who will believe them; faith is itself a warrant for trusting. If you can trust, you may trust. After being fulfilled hundreds of times, the words of promise still stand to be yet further made good. Many times and often, we have stooped down to the springhead in the meadow and sipped a cooling drink of water. It is just as full and free, and we may drink today with as much confidence as if we now stooped down to drink for the first time. People do not keep their same promise over and over again; it would be unreasonable to expect it of them. They are cisterns, but You, O Lord, are a fountain! All my fresh springs are in You.

Come and imitate Jacob! As he laid himself down in a certain place and took of the stones of the place for his pillows, you do the same. Here is the whole Bible for a couch, and here are certain promises to serve as pillows; lay down your burdens, and yourself also, and take your rest. Behold, this Scripture and its promises are from this point forward yours: *the land upon which thou dost lie, to thee will I give it.*

Chapter 15

Endorsing the Promise

I believe God, that it shall be even as it was told me. (Acts 27:25)

Paul had received a special promise, and he openly affirmed his faith in it. He believed that God would fulfill every detail of that promise. In this way, he demonstrated his belief that God is true. Each one of us is obligated to do this with those words of the Lord which are suitable to our case. This is what I mean by the chapter title of "Endorsing the Promise."

A friend might give me a check for the orphanage which says, "Pay to the order of C. H. Spurgeon the sum of $10." His name is good and his bank is good, but I get nothing from his kindness until I sign my own name on the back of his check. It is a very simple act. I simply sign my name, and the banker pays me; but this cannot be done without my signature.

There are many nobler names than mine, but none

of these can be used instead of my own. If I wrote the President's name, it would not help me. If the secretary of the treasury placed his signature on the back of the document, it would be useless. I must myself sign my own name. Even so, each person must personally accept, adopt, and endorse the promise of God by his own individual faith, or he will derive no benefit from it.

If you were to write a poem as good as those by John Milton in honor of the bank, or exceed Tennyson in verses in praise of the generous benefactor of the orphans, it would avail nothing. The finest language of men and of angels would count for nothing. What is absolutely required is the personal signature of the person who is named as the receiver. However fine might be the sketch which an artist's pencil might draw upon the back of the check, that also would be of no use. The simple, self-written name is demanded, and nothing will be accepted instead of it. We must each believe the promise for ourselves and declare that we know it to be true, or it will bring us no blessing. No good works, ceremonial performances, or exuberant feelings can supply the place of a simple confidence. *He that comes to God must believe that he is and that he is a rewarder of those that diligently seek him* (Hebrews 11:6). Some things may be or may not be, but this must be.

The promise may be said to be like this: "I promise to pay to the order of any sinner who will believe on Me the blessing of eternal life." The sinner must write his name on the back of the check, but nothing else is asked of him. He believes the promise, he goes to the throne of grace with it, and he looks to receive the mercy which it guaranteed to him. He will have that mercy; he cannot fail to do so. It is written, *He that believes in the Son has eternal life* (John 3:36); and so it is.

Paul believed that everyone in the ship with him would escape, because God had promised it. He accepted the promise as more than enough of a guarantee for the fact, and he acted accordingly. He was calm amid the storm. He gave his companions wise and sensible advice about breaking their fast. In general, he managed matters as a man would do who was sure of a happy escape from the tempest. So, he treated God as He should be treated –

> Our faithful God is jealous of His honor and cannot tolerate that men should treat Him as if He could be false.

with unquestioning confidence. An upright man likes to be trusted; it would grieve him if he saw that he was regarded with suspicion. Our faithful God is jealous of His honor and cannot tolerate that men should treat Him as if He could be false. Unbelief provokes the Lord above any other sin. It touches the apple of His eye and cuts Him to the quick. Far be it from us to perpetrate so infamous a wrong towards our heavenly Father; let us believe Him fully and unconditionally, placing no limits to our hearty reliance upon His Word.

Paul openly proclaimed his confidence in the promise. It is well that we should do the same. At this time, bold, outspoken testimonies to the truth of God are greatly needed and may prove to be of great value. The air is full of doubt; indeed, few people really and substantially believe. Such a man as George Müller, who believed in God for the care of two thousand children, is a rare person. *When the Son of man comes, shall he find faith on the earth?* (Luke 18:8). Therefore, let us speak out. Unbelief has defied us. Let no one's heart fail him, but let us meet the giant with the sling and stone of actual experience and unflinching witness. God keeps His promise, and we know it. We will endorse every one of His promises. Yes – we would do it with our blood if it were needful! The word of the Lord endures forever, and of this we are undaunted witnesses, even all of us who are called by His name.

Chapter 16

God's Provision for the Journey

Godliness is profitable unto all things, having promise of the life that now is and of that which is to come. (1 Timothy 4:8)

A sort of artificialness prevents some Christians from treating religion as if it has a place in everyday life. It is to them mystical and dreamy, or more like a work of religious fiction than a matter of truth and fact. They sort of believe in God, just for things spiritual and for the life which is to come; but they totally forget that true godliness has the promise of the life which now is, as well as of that which is to come. To them it would seem almost sacrilegious to pray about the small matters of which daily life is made up. Perhaps they will be startled if I try to suggest that this should make them question the reality of their faith. If it cannot bring them help in the little troubles of life, will it support them in the greater trials of death? If it cannot help them regarding food and clothing, what can it do for them regarding their immortal spirit?

In the life of Abraham, we perceive that his faith had to do with all the events of his earthly pilgrimage. It was connected to his moving from one country to another, to the separation of a nephew from his camp, to fighting against invaders, and especially to the birth of the long-promised son. No part of the patriarch's life was outside the circle of his faith in God. Toward the close of his life it is said, *and the LORD had blessed Abraham in all things* (Genesis 24:1), which included material things as well as spiritual. In Jacob's case, the Lord promised him bread to eat, clothing to wear, and that He would bring him to his father's house in peace. All these things are of a temporal and earthly character.

Certainly, these first believers did not run away with the present blessings of the covenant or regard it as a flippant, mystical matter to believe in God. One is struck with the lack of any line of division between secular and sacred in their lives. They journeyed as pilgrims, fought like Crusaders, ate and drank like saints, lived as priests, and spoke as prophets. Their life was their religion, and their religion was their life. They trusted God, not merely about certain things of greater importance, but about everything. That is why even a servant from one of their houses, when he was sent on an errand, prayed, *O LORD, God of my master Abraham, . . . prosper my way by which I go* (Genesis 24:42). This was genuine faith, and we ought to imitate it and no longer allow the substance of the promise and the life of faith to evaporate in mere sentimental and imaginative notions. If trust in God is good for anything, it is good for everything within the line of the promise, and it is certain that the life that now is, lies within that region.

Observe and use practically such words of God as these:

> *Ye shall serve the LORD your God, and he shall bless thy bread and thy water; and I will take all sickness away from the midst of thee.* (Exodus 23:25)

> *Wait in the LORD and do good; live in the land and uphold the truth.* (Psalm 37:3)

> *Surely he shall deliver thee from the snare of the fowler and from the mortal pestilence. He shall cover thee with his feathers, and under his wings thou shalt be secure: his truth shall be thy shield and buckler. Thou shalt not be afraid for the terror by night, nor for the arrow that flies by day, nor for the pestilence that walks in darkness, nor for the destruction that wastes at noonday. Thousands shall fall at thy side and ten thousands at thy right hand, but it shall not come near thee.* (Psalm 91:3-7)

> *He shall deliver thee in six tribulations, and in the seventh no evil shall touch thee.* (Job 5:19)

> *He that walks in righteousness, he that*

speaks uprightly; he that despises the gain of violence, he that shakes his hands from receiving bribes; he that stops his ears to not hear of blood; he who shuts his eyes to not see evil; he shall dwell upon the high places: fortresses of rocks shall be his place of refuge: bread shall be given him; his waters shall be sure. (Isaiah 33:15-16)

For the LORD God is a sun and shield unto us; the LORD will give grace and glory; he will not withhold good from those that walk uprightly. (Psalm 84:11)

No weapon that is formed against thee shall prosper; and every tongue that shall rise against thee in judgment thou shalt condemn. This is the heritage of the slaves of the LORD, and their justice from me, said the LORD. (Isaiah 54:17)

Our Savior intended faith to calm us regarding our daily cares, or He would not have said, *Therefore I say unto you, Take no thought for your life, what ye shall eat or what ye shall drink, nor yet for your body, what ye shall put on. Is not the life more than food, and the body than raiment? Behold the fowls of the air, for they sow not, neither do they reap nor gather into barns, yet your heavenly Father feeds them. Are ye not much better than they?* (Matthew 6:25-26). What else but the exercise of faith concerning earthly things could He have meant when He used the following language: *And seek not what ye shall eat or what ye shall drink, neither be ye high minded. For all these things do the Gentiles of the world seek after, and your Father knows that ye have need of these things* (Luke 12:29-30)?

Paul meant the same when he wrote, *Be anxious for nothing, but in every thing by prayer and supplication with thanksgiving, let your requests be made known unto God. And the peace of God, which passes all understanding, shall keep your hearts and minds through Christ Jesus* (Philippians 4:6-7).

He who has gone to prepare heaven for us will not leave us without provision for the journey there. God does not renegotiate on His heavenly offer. God makes the road, as well as the end, certain and secure.

> He who has gone to prepare heaven for us will not leave us without provision for the journey there.

Our earthly necessities are as real as our spiritual ones, and we may be sure that the Lord will supply them. He will send us those supplies in the way of promise, prayer, and faith, and so make them a means of education for us. He will prepare us for Canaan by the experience of the wilderness.

To suppose that earthly things are too little for our great God is to forget that He observes the flight of sparrows and counts the hairs of our head. Besides, everything is so little to Him that if He does not care for the little things, He cares for nothing. Who is to divide matters by size or weight? The turning point of history may be a small circumstance. Blessed is the man to whom nothing is too small for God; for certainly nothing is too small to cause us sorrow or to involve us in danger.

A man of God once lost a key. He prayed about it and found it. He spoke about that as a strange circumstance, but indeed, it was nothing unusual for God.

Some of us pray about everything, and we tremble lest we forget to sanctify even the smallest thing by the Word of God and prayer. It is not *including* the trivial things that troubles our consciences, but *omitting* them. We are assured that when our Lord gave His angels charge to guard our feet from stones in the way, He placed all the details of our life under heavenly care, and we are glad to commit all things to His keeping.

It is one of the abiding miracles of the present age that in Christ we have continual peace under all trials, and through Him we have power in prayer to obtain from the Lord all things necessary for this life and godliness. It has been my experience in life to test the Lord hundreds of times about earthly needs, being driven to prayer by the care of orphans and students. Prayer has many, many times brought suitable supplies and cleared away serious difficulties. I know that faith can fill a wallet, provide a meal, change a hard heart, obtain a site for a building, heal sickness, quiet rebellion, and restrain an epidemic. Like money in the hand of a person in this world, faith in the hand of a person of God *answers all things* (Ecclesiastes 10:19). All things in heaven and earth and under the earth answer to the command of prayer. Faith is not to be imitated by a con man nor simulated by a hypocrite, but where it is real and can grasp a divine promise with a firm grip, it is a great wonder-worker.

How I wish that you would so believe in God as to lean upon Him in all the concerns of this life! This would lead you into a new world and bring to you such affirming evidence as to the truth of our holy faith that you would laugh sceptics to scorn. Childlike faith in God provides sincere hearts with practical prudence, which I am inclined to call sanctified common sense. The simple-minded believer, though mocked as a fool, has a wisdom about him which comes from above and effectually confounds the guile of the wicked. Nothing puzzles a malicious enemy like the straightforward unguardedness of an out-and-out believer.

He who believes in His God *shall not be afraid of evil rumours; his heart is fixed, trusting in the LORD* (Psalm 112:7). In a thousand ways this faith sweetens, enlarges, and enriches life. Try it, and see if it does not yield for you an immeasurable wealth of blessedness! It will not save you from trouble, for the promise is, *These things I have spoken unto you that in me ye might have peace. In the world ye shall have tribulation; but be of good cheer; I have overcome the world* (John 16:33). It will cause you to glory in tribulations also, *knowing that the tribulation works patience; and patience, experience; and experience, hope; and the hope shall not be ashamed, because the love of God is poured out in our hearts by the Holy Spirit which is given unto us* (Romans 5:3-5).

My faith not only flies to heaven,
    But walks with God below;
To me are all things daily given,
    While passing to and fro.

The promise speaks of worlds above,
    But not of these alone;
It feeds and clothes me *now* with love,
    And makes this world my own.

I trust the Lord, and he replies,
    In things both great and small.
He honors faith with prompt supplies;
    Faith honors *him* in all.[6]

---

6   Author Unknown

Chapter 17

Searching Out the Promise

Thou hast spoken this goodness unto thy slave. (2 Samuel 7:28)

King David knew what the Lord had promised to give him, and he referred to it especially in his prayer as *this good thing* (Revised Standard Version). We greatly need to be more deliberate and specific in our supplications than we usually are. We pray for everything in such a way that we practically pray for nothing. It is good to know what we need. That is why our Lord said to the blind man, *What wilt thou that I should do unto thee?* (Mark 10:51). Jesus wanted him to be aware of his own needs and to be filled with earnest desires concerning those needs. These are valuable ingredients in the composition of prayer.

After realizing what we need, our next business is to find that the Lord has promised us this particular blessing, for then we can go to God with the utmost confidence and look for the fulfillment of His word. To this end, we should diligently search the Scriptures, looking much to the cases of other believers which are like our own, and attempting to find that particular utterance of divine grace which is suitable to ourselves in our present circumstances. The more exact the agreement of the promise to our specific case, the greater the comfort which will result.

In this school, the believer will learn the value of plenary, or verbal, inspiration – that every word in the Word is intended and inspired by God. In your own circumstance, you might have to dwell upon so slight a matter as the number of a noun, as Paul did when quoting the promise made to Abraham. Paul remarks, *Now to Abraham and his seed were the promises made. He did not say, And to seeds, as of many, but as of one, And to thy seed, which is Christ* (Galatians 3:16).

We may rest assured that somewhere in the inspired pages of the Bible there is a promise fitting the occasion. The infinite wisdom of God is seen in His having given us a revelation which meets the innumerable varieties of His people's conditions. Not a single trial is overlooked, however unusual it may be. As there is food especially adapted for every living thing upon the face of the earth, so there is suitable support for every child of God in the Word of God. If we do not find a relevant promise, it is because we do not look for it, or having found it, we have not yet perceived its full meaning.

A simple comparison may be useful here. You have lost the key to an old chest, and after trying all the keys you can find, you have no other option but to send for a locksmith. The tradesman comes with a huge bunch of keys of all sorts and sizes. To you they appear to be one big collection of rusty instruments. He looks at the lock, and then he tries first one key and then another. He has not opened it yet, and your treasures are still out of your reach. Now he has found a likely key. It almost touches the bolt, but not quite. He is evidently on the right track now. At last, the chest is opened, for the right key has been found.

This is a correct representation of many difficulties. You cannot get at the difficulty so as to deal with it properly and find your way to a happy result. You pray, but have not the liberty in prayer which you desire. A definite promise is what you need. You try one and another of the inspired words, but they do not fit. The troubled heart sees reasons to suspect that they are not strictly applicable to the case in hand, and so they are left in the old Book for use

> **If we do not find a relevant promise, it is because we do not look for it, or having found it, we have not yet perceived its full meaning.**

on another day, for they are not available in the present emergency. You try again, and in due season a promise presents itself which seems to have been made for the occasion. It fits as exactly as a well-made key fits the area of the lock for which it was originally prepared. Having found the identical word of the living God, you hurry to plead it at the throne of grace, saying, "O my Lord, You have promised this good thing unto Your servant; be pleased to grant it!" The matter is ended. Sorrow is turned to joy. Your prayer is heard.

Frequently, the Holy Spirit brings words of the Lord to our remembrance with life and power, which we might otherwise have forgotten. He also sheds a new light upon well-remembered passages, and so reveals a fullness in them which we had little suspected. In cases known to me, the texts have seemed puzzling, and for a while, the person upon whose mind they were impressed could hardly see their meaning. For years, one heart was comforted with the words *His soul shall rest in that which is good; and his seed shall inherit the earth* (Psalm 25:13). This passage was seldom out of his mind; indeed, it seemed to him to be perpetually whispered in his ear. The special relation of the promise to his experience was made known by the event. Another time, a child of God, who mourned his years of difficulty and lack of success, was lifted at once into joy and peace by that seldom-quoted word, *I will restore to you the years that the caterpillar has eaten* (Joel 2:25). The bitter experiences of David regarding slander and malice led to the utterance of comforting promises which have been a thousand times appropriated by lonely and brokenhearted Christians when afflicted with *cruel mockings and scourgings* (Hebrews 11:36).

Before this age will end, we are confident that every sentence of Scripture will have been illustrated by the life of one or another of the saints. Perhaps some obscure and little-understood promise is still waiting until he shall come for whom it was especially written. If we may say so, there is one rusty key on the bunch which has not yet found its lock, but it will find it before the history of the church is finished. We may be sure of that.

The word of the Lord which would remove our present discomfort may be close at hand, and yet we may not be aware of it. With extraordinary knowledge of human experience, John Bunyan, in his book *The Pilgrim's Progress*, represents the prisoner of Doubting Castle as finding in his own possession the key called Promise, which opened every door in that gloomy prison house. We often lie in dismal confinement while the means of obtaining full liberty offers itself to us. If we would but open our eyes, we would, like Hagar, see a well of water close at hand, and wonder why we thought of dying of thirst (see Genesis 21:19).

At this moment, O tempted brother, there is a word of the Lord awaiting you! As the manna fell early in the morning and lay ready for the Israelites to gather it as soon as they left their beds (Exodus 16), so does the promise of the Lord wait for your coming. The oxen and the young animals of grace are killed, and all things are ready for your immediate comfort (Matthew 22:4). The mountain is full of chariots of fire and horses of fire, prepared for your deliverance (2 Kings 6:15-17). The prophet of the Lord can see them, and if your eyes were opened, you would see them too. Like the lepers at the gate of Samaria, it would be foolish for you to sit where you are and die (2 Kings 7:3-4). Rise up, for lavish mercy is poured forth nearby, exceeding abundantly above all that you ask or even think (Ephesians 3:20). Only believe, and enter into rest (Hebrews 4:3).

For the poor, the sick, the weak, and the wandering,

there are words of good cheer which they alone can enjoy. For the fallen, the discouraged, the despairing, and the dying, there are remedies which are made for their specific ailment. The widow and the fatherless have their promises, and so do captives, travelers, shipwrecked mariners, the elderly, and those who are at the moment of death. No one ever wanders where a promise does not follow him. An atmosphere of promise surrounds believers just like the air surrounds the globe. I might almost call it omnipresent and say of it, *Thou hast formed my face and my insides and laid thine hand upon me. Thy knowledge is wonderful beyond my ability to comprehend; it is high, I cannot understand it. Where shall I go from thy spirit? or where shall I flee from thy presence?* (Psalm 139:5-7).

No depth of darkness can hide us from the covenant of promise; rather, in its presence the night shines as the day. Therefore, let us take courage, and by faith and patience wait in the land of our exile until the day we are brought home. Then we will, like the rest of the heirs of salvation, *inherit the promises* (Hebrews 6:12).

Certain covenant agreements made with the Lord Jesus Christ concerning His elect and redeemed ones are completely without condition as far as we are concerned; but many other well-supplied words of the Lord contain stipulations which must be carefully regarded, or we will not obtain the specific blessing. Part of your diligent search must be directed toward this most crucial point. God will keep His promise to you, but be sure to carefully observe the way it is worded and any conditions involved. Only when we fulfill the requirement of a conditional promise can we expect that promise to be fulfilled to us.

He has said, *Believe on the Lord Jesus Christ, and thou shalt be saved* (Acts 16:31). If you believe in the Lord Jesus Christ, it is certain that you will be saved; but you must believe. In the same way, if the promise is made regarding prayer, holiness, reading the Word, abiding in Christ, or whatever else it may be, give your heart and soul to the thing commanded, that the blessing may become yours. In some cases, great blessedness is not realized because known duties are neglected.

> In some cases, great blessedness is not realized because known duties are neglected.

The promise cannot enter if *sin lies at the door* (Genesis 4:7). Even an unknown duty may whip us with a *few stripes* (Luke 12:48), and a few strokes may greatly impair our happiness. Let us strive to know the Lord's will in all things, and then let us obey it without a trace of hesitation. It is not about the road of our willfulness, but about the path of divine wisdom that we read, *Her ways are ways of pleasantness, and all her paths are peace* (Proverbs 3:17).

Do not undervalue the grace of the promise because it has a condition attached to it. As a rule, it is in this way made twice as valuable. The condition itself is another blessing, which the Lord has purposely made inseparable from that which you desire, that you may gain two mercies while seeking only one. Moreover, remember that the condition is grievous only to those who are not heirs of the promise. To them it is as a thorn hedge, keeping them from the comfort to which they have no right; but to you it is not grievous, but pleasant, and it is therefore no hindrance to your access to the blessing. Those requirements which show a black cloud and darkness to the Egyptians have a bright side for the Israelites and give light by night to them (Exodus 14:20). To us, the Lord's yoke is easy, and in taking it upon us we find rest unto our souls (Matthew 11:28-30). See, then, that you pay attention to the wording of the promise. Carry out all its precepts, that all good things may come to you.

If you are a believer in the Lord Jesus, all the promises are yours, and among them is one for this very day and for the particular place where you are in life. Therefore, search the Scriptures and find your portion for this hour. Of all the promises which the Lord has given in His Book, He has said, *Seek ye out that which is written in the book of the LORD and read; if one of these is lacking, none is missing with his mate, for his mouth has commanded it, and his same Spirit has gathered them* (Isaiah 34:16). Therefore, trust, and do not be afraid. Whatever else may prove a failure, the promise of God never will. Treasure laid up in this bank is beyond all risk. *It is better to trust in the LORD than to put confidence in princes* (Psalm 118:9). Let us sing at every remembrance of the God of truth and grace.

Tell of His wondrous faithfulness
    And sound His power abroad;
Sing the sweet promise of His grace,
    And the performing God.

He that can dash whole worlds to death,
    And make them when He please,
He speaks, and that almighty breath
    Fulfils His great decrees.

His very word of grace is strong
    As that which built the skies;
The voice that rolls the stars along
    Speaks all the promises.[7]

---

7   From the hymn "Begin, My Tongue, Some Heav'nly Theme," by Isaac Watts

Chapter 18

The Timing of the Promise

The time of the promise drew nigh. (Acts 7:17)

Thomas Brooks reminds us that the mercies of God are not called *swift*, but certain, or sure: *the sure mercies of David* (Isaiah 55:3). There is nothing about being in a hurry in the way the Lord works. It may even seem that the chariots of His grace are slow in coming. It is by no means an unusual circumstance for the saints to be heard crying, *O LORD, how long?* (Habakkuk 1:2; Psalm 13:1-2). It is written that *the glory of the LORD shall gather thee* (Isaiah 58:8). The rear guard comes up last, but it does come. God may sometimes make us wait, but we will see in the end that He is as surely the Omega as the Alpha of His people's salvation. Let us never doubt Him. Though the answer is delayed, let us wait for it. It will surely come. *For the vision is yet for an appointed time, but at the end it shall speak and not lie; though it tarry, wait for it because it will surely come; wait for it* (Habakkuk 2:3).

A ship once sailed from the port of London, which the owner called the *Swift-sure*, because he hoped it would prove both safe and speedy. Truly, this is a proper name for the Lord's mercy. It is both swift and sure. David may not have said so in the text which Thomas Brooks quotes, but he often said as much and even more in others. David wrote that God *rode upon a cherub and flew: yea, he flew upon the wings of the wind* (Psalm 18:10).

The Lord is not slow to hear the cries of His people. He has a set time to favor Zion, and when that set time is come, there will be no delay.

The date for its fulfillment is an important part of a promise. Indeed, it enters into the essence of it. It would be unjust to delay the payment of a debt, and the obligation to keep one's word is of the same nature. The Lord is prompt to the moment in carrying out His gracious promises.

The Lord had threatened to destroy the world with a flood, but He delayed until the last moment until Noah had entered the ark; and then *the same day were all the fountains of the great deep broken up, and the windows of the heavens were opened* (Genesis 7:11). God had declared that Israel should come out of Egypt, and it was so. *And it came to pass at the end of the four hundred and thirty years, even that same day it came to pass, that all the hosts of the LORD went out from the land of Egypt* (Exodus 12:41). According to Daniel, the Lord numbers the years of His promise and counts the weeks of His waiting (see Daniel 9:2, 24-27). As for the greatest promise of all – the sending of His Son from heaven – the Lord was not behind in delivering that great gift, *but when the fullness of the time was come, God sent forth his Son, born of a woman* (Galatians 4:4). Beyond all question, the Lord our God keeps His word to the moment.

When we are in need, we may be urgent with the Lord to come quickly to our rescue, even as David pleaded in the seventieth psalm: *Make haste, O God, to deliver me; make haste to help me, O LORD. I am poor and destitute; make haste unto me, O God: thou art my help and my deliverer; O LORD, make no tarrying* (Psalm 70:1, 5). The Lord even describes Himself as hurrying to carry out His

Beyond all question, the Lord our God keeps His word to the moment.

gracious engagements when it pleases Him, saying, *I the LORD will hasten it in its time* (Isaiah 60:22). We must not pray in this way, however, as if we had the slightest fear that the Lord could or would be slow, or that He needed us to help Him hurry His response. No. *The Lord is not late concerning his promise, as some count lateness* (2 Peter 3:9). Our God is slow to anger, but in deeds of grace *his word runs very swiftly* (Psalm 147:15). Sometimes His speed to bless His people outstrips time and thought, as, for example, when He fulfills that ancient declaration, *And it shall come to pass, that before they call, I will answer; and while they are yet speaking, I will hear* (Isaiah 65:24).

Yet there are delays in the answers to our prayers. As

the farmer does not reap today that which he planted yesterday, neither do we always immediately obtain from the Lord that which we seek from Him. The door of grace does open, but not always to our first knocks. Why is this? It is because the mercy will be all the greater for being longer on the road. There is a time for every purpose under heaven, and everything is best in its time (see Ecclesiastes 3). Fruit ripens in its season, and the more seasonable it is, the better it is. Untimely mercies would be only half mercies; therefore, the Lord withholds them until they have come to their perfection. Even heaven itself will be all the better because it will not be ours until it is prepared for us and we are prepared for it.

Love presides over the arrangements of grace and strikes upon the bell when the best moment has arrived. God blesses us by His temporary delays, as well as by His prompt replies. We are not to doubt the Lord because His time has not yet come. That would be to act like spoiled children who must have something at that moment, or else they think they will never have it.

A waiting God is the true object of confidence to His waiting people. *Therefore will the LORD wait for you, that he may have mercy on you* (Isaiah 30:18). His compassions will not fail, even when His gracious operations appear to be suspended and our distress has increased. It is because He loves us so much that He tests us by delaying His answers of peace. It is with our Father in heaven even as it was with our Lord on earth: *Now Jesus loved Martha and her sister and Lazarus. When he had heard therefore that he was sick, he abode two days still in the same place where he was* (John 11:5-6). Love sometimes closes the hand of divine bounty and restrains the outflow of favor when it sees that we will benefit from a period of trial.

Perhaps the time of the promise has not yet come because our trial has not yet fulfilled its design. The chastening must answer its purpose or it cannot be brought to an end. Who would desire to see the gold taken out of the fire before its dross is consumed? Wait, O precious thing, until you have gained

> These furnace moments are profitable.

the utmost purity! These furnace moments are profitable. It would be unwise to shorten such golden hours. The time of the promise corresponds with the time most enriching to heart and soul.

Moreover, we might not have displayed sufficient submission to the divine will. Patience has not yet had her perfect work. The weaning process is not accomplished. We might still desire the comforts which the Lord intends us forever to outgrow. Abraham made a great feast when his son Isaac was weaned, and it may be that our heavenly Father will do the same with us. Lie down, proud heart! Put away your idols. Forsake your fondness for the things of this world, and the promised peace will come to you.

It might also be that we have not yet performed a duty which will become the turning point of our condition. The Lord turned again the captivity of Job when he prayed for his friends (Job 42:10). It may be that the Lord will make us useful to a relative or other friend before He will favor us with personal consolations. We are not to see the face of our Joseph except our brother be with us (see Genesis 44:26). Some ordinance of the Lord's house may lie neglected or some holy work may be left undone, and this may hinder the promise. Is it so? *Are the consolations of God in such small esteem with thee? Is there by chance any secret thing concerning thee?* (Job 15:11). Maybe God is waiting for us to make a promise to Him or a notable sacrifice for Him, and then He will bring His covenant to mind. Let Him not have to complain that *Thou hast bought me no sweet cane with money* (Isaiah 43:24). Rather, let us accept His challenge: *Bring ye all the tithes into the storehouse, that there may be meat in mine house, and prove me now herewith, saith the LORD of hosts, if I will not open you the windows of heaven, and pour you out a blessing* (Malachi 3:10).

God's promises are so timed as to secure His glory in their fulfillment, and this must be good enough for us when we can see no other reason for delay. It might be necessary for us to be made more fully aware of our need and the great value of the blessings which we crave. That which comes too lightly may be too lightly prized. Perhaps our ungrateful spirits need to be taught to be thankful by an education of waiting. We might not loudly sing if we did not deeply sigh. Wanting and waiting lead to thirsting and pleading, and these in due time lead to joy and rejoicing.

If all things could be known to us as they are known to God, we would bless Him with all our hearts for keeping us under His discipline and for not sparing us because we cried. If we could know the end as well as the beginning, we would praise the Lord for closed doors and frowning looks and unanswered petitions. Certainly, if we knew that the Lord's great purposes were answered by our continuing without the pleasures we desire and by our bearing the evils which we dread, we would cry aloud to be left in our poverty and to be confined in our pain. If we can glorify God by being denied what we seek, then we desire to be denied. The greatest of all our prayers and the sum of all the rest is this one: *Nevertheless not as I will, but as thou wilt* (Matthew 26:39).

Chapter 19

The Seal of the Holy Spirit

That Holy Spirit of the promise, which is the earnest of our inheritance unto the redemption of the purchased possession, unto the praise of his glory. (Ephesians 1:13-14)

In a very true and real sense, the things promised in the covenant are already the property of believers. *All things are yours* (1 Corinthians 3:21). The great Father might truly say to each one of the sons who abides in His house, *All that I have is thine* (Luke 15:31). The inheritance is already ours, say the old preachers, *in promisso, in pretio, in principiis*, that is to say, in the promise of God, in the price paid by the Lord Jesus, and in its first principles which are infused into us by the Holy Spirit. In His unfailing promise, the Father has already *blessed us with all spiritual blessings in heavenly things in Christ* (Ephesians 1:3). He has not only resolved to enrich us in the future, but even now

143

He has also blessed us with the treasures of His love. The Lord Jesus has not merely made us heirs of an infinite estate in the ages to come, but He has brought us into immediate enjoyment of a present portion, as the Scriptures say: *In whom likewise we have obtained an inheritance* (Ephesians 1:11).

The Holy Spirit is in many ways the means of making the promised heritage ours even now. By him we are "sealed" (Ephesians 1:13). We know for certain that the inheritance is ours, and that we ourselves belong to the great Heir of all things. The workings of the Holy Spirit upon us in our regeneration, and His abiding in us by sanctification, are the authentication of our being in grace and of our being inheritors of glory. Beyond all other testimonies of our being saved, there stands sure and certain evidence, namely, that the Spirit of the living God rests upon us.

Repentance, faith, spiritual life, holy desires, upward breathings, and even *groanings which cannot be uttered* (Romans 8:26) are all proofs that the Holy Spirit is working upon us, and working in a way specific to the heirs of salvation. Life breathed into us by the Holy Spirit is the great seal of the kingdom of God to our souls. The Spirit of promise does not prepare us for a blessedness which will never be ours. He who has worked in us to prepare us for something will secure that blessing to us for which He has prepared us. The faintest impress of the seal of the Spirit is a better witness of our part and parcel with the people of God than all the bold assumptions which self-conceit can draw from its spirited notions.

Not only is the Holy Spirit the seal of the inheritance, but He is also the assurance or earnest of it. An earnest is a part of the thing itself, given as a guarantee that the remainder will be forthcoming in due season. If a man is paid part of his wage in the middle of the week, it is earnest money. In this an earnest differs from a pledge, for a pledge is returned when we receive that which it secured; but an earnest is not returned, for it is a part of that which is promised. Even so, the Holy Spirit is Himself a great portion of the inheritance of the saints, and in having Him we have the beginning of perfectness, of heaven, and of eternal glory. He is everlasting life, and His gifts, graces, and workings are the first principles of endless joy. In having the Holy Spirit, we have the kingdom, which it is our Father's good pleasure to give to His chosen people.

Heaven will much consist of holiness, and it is clear that, as far as the Holy Spirit makes us holy here, He has implanted the beginnings of heaven.

This will be made clear by a few moments' reflection. Heaven will much consist of holiness, and it is clear that, as far as the Holy Spirit makes us holy here, He has implanted the beginnings of heaven. Heaven is victory, and each time we overcome sin, Satan, the world, and the flesh, we have foretastes of the unfading triumph which causes the waving of palms in the New Jerusalem. Heaven is an endless Sabbath, and how can we have better foretastes of the perfect rest than by that joy and peace which are shed abroad in us by the Holy Spirit?

Communion with God is a main ingredient in the joy of the glorified; and here below, by the Spirit of God, we are enabled to delight ourselves in the Lord and rejoice in the God of our salvation (Psalm 37:4; Habakkuk 3:18). Fellowship with the Lord Jesus in all His gracious designs and purposes, and likeness to Him in love for God and man, are also main ingredients in our perfected condition before the throne; and the Spirit of holiness is forming these in us from day to day. To be pure in heart so as to see God, to be established in character so as to be established in righteousness, to be strong in good so as to overcome all evil, and to be cleansed from self so as to find our all in God – are not these, when carried to the full, among the central benedictions of the Beatitudes (Matthew 5:3-11)? And are they not already bestowed upon us by that Spirit of glory and power which even now rests upon us? It is so. In the Holy Spirit we have the things we seek after. In Him, the flower of heaven has come to us in the bud, and the dawn of the day of glory has smiled upon us.

We are not, then, such strangers to the promised blessings as common talk would make us out to be. Many, like parrots, repeat the word, *That which eye has not seen nor ear heard neither has entered into the heart of man is that which God has prepared for those that love him* (1 Corinthians 2:9), but they fail to add the words that follow: *But God has revealed this unto us by his Spirit* (1 Corinthians 2:10). What cruelty it is to cut the living child of Scripture in half! The Holy Spirit has revealed to us what neither eye nor ear has perceived. He has drawn back the curtains and allowed us to see the secrets hidden from ages and from generations. In the life of God within your soul dwells the everlasting life which is promised to those who love God. The life of glory is the continuance and the outgrowth of the life of grace.

In reconciliation through the atoning blood, behold that celestial peace which is the groundwork of eternal rest. Get a foretaste of the fragrance of delight in the love of God shed abroad in the believing soul. Observe, in the steadfast security and sacred serenity of full assurance, a forecast of the infinite rest of paradise. When our inward joys rise high and burst into a song, then we hear preludes of the heavenly hallelujahs. If we want to know the clusters of the fruit of Canaan, behold, they are brought to us by those emotions and anticipations which, under the guidance of the Spirit, have gone like spies into the good land and brought us its choicest fruits (see Numbers 13:16-26)!

It is not only that we will have an inheritance, but also that we have it now. In having the Holy Spirit, we are already in possession of the land which flows with milk and honey (see Numbers 13:27). *We who have believed do enter into the rest* (Hebrews 4:3). *Ye are come unto Mount Sion and unto the city of the living God, the heavenly Jerusalem, and to an innumerable company of angels* (Hebrews 12:22).

What remains for such people to do who have been made partakers of a divine inheritance in the Son of God, but to walk worthy of their high, holy, and heavenly calling. *If ye then are risen with Christ, seek those things which are above, where the Christ sits at the right hand of God* (Colossians 3:1).

Chapter 20

The Lord Jesus Christ and the Promises

For all the promises of God are yes in him,
and in him Amen, by us for the glory of God.
(2 Corinthians 1:20)

Jesus, our Lord, stands forever connected to the way of the promise. Indeed, He is *the way, the truth, and the life* (John 14:6). No man comes to the Faithful Promiser but by Jesus Christ. We could not close this little book without a short chapter about Him. Our hope is that you will not attempt to obtain any comfort from a word that we have written, or even from the Word of God itself, except as you receive it through Jesus Christ. Apart from Him, the Scripture itself contains nothing upon which the soul of man may live.

This, indeed, is the great fault of many. They search the Scriptures, for in them they think they have eternal life (John 5:39), but they will not come unto Christ that they might have life (John 5:40). Let us not be part of this foolish group, but let us come to Jesus day by day, knowing that it pleased the Father that in Him should all fullness dwell (Colossians 1:19). Only as we know Him do we know the light, life, and liberty of the heirs of promise; and, as surely as we wander from Him, we roam into bondage. Oh, for grace to abide in Him, that we may possess all the good things of the covenant made with us in Him!

Jesus is the gate of the promises. Through Him, the Lord is able to enter into gracious commitments with guilty people. Until "the seed of the woman" had been appointed to be the mediator between God and man (1 Timothy 2:5), no messages of comfort could be sent to those who cause the offense. God had no word for sinners until the Word of God *was made flesh and dwelt among us* (John 1:14). God could not communicate His mind of love to us except through Jesus, the Word. As God could not come to us apart from the messenger of the covenant, so we could not approach Him except through Jesus, the Mediator. Our fears drive us away from the Holy One until we see in the Son of God a brother full of tender sympathy. The glory of the divine Trinity overawes us until we behold the milder radiance of the incarnate God. We come to God through the humanity of His Son, and especially through that humanity, suffering and dying on our behalf.

Jesus is the sum of all the promises. When God promised His Son to be ours, He gave us in Him all things necessary for our salvation. Every good gift and every perfect gift will be found within the person, offices, and work of our Redeemer. All the promises are in Him. If you would like to add them up or make a long list of all the blessings which they secure to us, you may save yourself the trouble and be happy to know that this is the full total: the Lord has given us His Son, Jesus. As all the stars are in the sky and all the waves are in the sea, so are all covenant blessings in Christ. There is no real blessing outside of our Lord. He is all in all. This string holds all the pearls. This jewelry box holds all the gems.

Jesus is the guarantee of the promises. He who did not spare His own Son will deny nothing to His people. If He had ever thought of drawing back, He would have done so before He had made the infinite sacrifice of His only begotten Son. There can never be a suspicion that the Lord will revoke any one of the promises, since He has already fulfilled the greatest and most costly of them all.

> **There can never be a suspicion that the Lord will revoke any one of the promises, since He has already fulfilled the greatest and most costly of them all.**

He that did not spare his own Son, but delivered him up for us all, how shall he not also give us all things with him? (Romans 8:32).

Jesus is the confirmer of the promises. They *are yes in him, and in him Amen* (2 Corinthians 1:20). His coming into our nature, His standing as our Head, and His fulfilling of all the stipulations of the covenant, have made all the articles of the divine compact firm and enduring. Now it is not only kind, but it is also just with God to keep His promises to men. Since Jesus has provided, on our behalf, full restitution to the divine honor that sin has assailed, the justice of God unites with His love in securing the carrying out of every word of promise.

As the rainbow is our assurance that the world will never again be destroyed by a flood (Genesis 9:12-17), so Jesus is our assurance that the floods of human sin will never drown the faithful kindness of the Lord. He has magnified the law and made it honorable. He must be rewarded for His soul's travail, and therefore all good things must come to those for whom He died. It would be an unhinging and dislocation of all things if the promises were now to become of no effect after our Lord has done all that was required to make them sure. If we are indeed one with the Lord Jesus Christ, the promises are as sure to us as the love of His Father is to Him.

Jesus is the one who makes remembrance of the promises. He pleads with God on our behalf, and His plea is the divine promise. He *made intercession for the transgressors* (Isaiah 53:12). For the good things that He has promised, the Lord will be inquired of by us that He may do them for us; and that this inquiry may be carried out under the most encouraging circumstances, behold, the Lord Jesus Himself becomes the Intercessor for us. For Zion's sake He does not hold His peace (Isaiah 62:1), but day and night He makes remembrance of the everlasting covenant and of the blood by which it was sealed and ratified. At the back of every promise stands the living, pleading, and prevailing High Priest of our faith. We may forget the faithful promise, but He will not. He will present the incense of His merit and the promises of God on our behalf, in that place within the veil where He exercises omnipotent intercession.

Jesus is the fulfiller of the promises. His first coming brought us the major part of the blessings which the Lord has foreordained for His own, and His second coming is to bring us the rest. Our spiritual riches are linked with His ever-endearing person. Because He lives, we live. Because He reigns, we reign. Because He is accepted, we are accepted. Soon, at His manifestation, we will be manifested. In His triumph, we will triumph. In His glory, we will be glorified.

> Nothing is too good for the Father to give to the person who delights in His Son, Jesus.

He is Himself the Alpha and the Omega of the promises of God. In Him we have found life as sinners, and in Him we will find glory as saints. If He is not risen, our faith is vain. If He does not come a second time, our hope is a delusion; but, since He has risen from the dead, we are justified. Since He will come in the glory of the Father, we will also be glorified.

What will you do with Christ?

All will depend upon your answer to this question. Do you rest in Him alone? If so, then the Lord has promised to bless you and to do good to you, and He will surprise you with the amazing manner in which He will do this for you. Nothing is too good for the Father to give to the person who delights in His Son, Jesus.

On the other hand, are you trusting in your own works, feelings, prayers, and traditions? Then you are of the works of the law and you are under the curse of the law. Remember what was said about the descendants of Hagar, the bondwoman, and you can determine what your share will be. Oh, that you would leave the house of bondage and flee to the home of free grace, and become one whom God will bless – according to the PROMISE!

May God grant this great favor unto you for the Lord Jesus Christ's sake! Amen.

About the Author

Charles Haddon Spurgeon was born on June 19, 1834, in Kelvedon, Essex, England. He was one of seventeen children in his family (nine of whom died in infancy). His father and grandfather were Nonconformist ministers in England. Due to economic difficulties, eighteen-month-old Charles was sent to live with his grandfather, who helped teach Charles the ways of God. Later in life, Charles remembered looking at the pictures in *Pilgrim's Progress* and in *Foxe's Book of Martyrs* as a young boy.

Charles did not have much of a formal education and never went to college. He read much throughout his life though, especially books by Puritan authors.

Even with godly parents and grandparents, young Charles resisted giving in to God. It was not until he was fifteen years old that he was born again. He was on his way to his usual church, but when a heavy snowstorm prevented him from getting there, he turned in at a little Primitive Methodist chapel. Though there were only about fifteen people in attendance, the preacher spoke from Isaiah 45:22: *Look unto me, and be ye saved, all the ends of the earth.* Charles Spurgeon's eyes were opened and the Lord converted his soul.

He began attending a Baptist church and teaching Sunday school. He soon preached his first sermon, and then when he was sixteen years old, he became the pastor of a small Baptist church in Cambridge. The church soon grew to over four hundred people, and Charles Spurgeon, at the age of nineteen, moved on to become the pastor of the New Park Street Church in London. The church grew from a few hundred attenders to a few thousand. They built an addition to the church, but still needed more room to accommodate the congregation. The Metropolitan Tabernacle was built in London in 1861, seating more than 5,000 people. Pastor Spurgeon preached the simple message of the cross, and thereby attracted many people who wanted to hear God's Word preached in the power of the Holy Spirit.

On January 9, 1856, Charles married Susannah Thompson. They had twin boys, Charles and Thomas. Charles and Susannah loved each other deeply, even amidst the difficulties and troubles that they faced in life, including health problems. They helped each other spiritually, and often together read the writings of

Jonathan Edwards, Richard Baxter, and other Puritan writers.

Charles Spurgeon was a friend of all Christians, but he stood firmly on the Scriptures, and it didn't please all who heard him. Spurgeon believed in and preached on the sovereignty of God, heaven and hell, repentance, revival, holiness, salvation through Jesus Christ alone, and the infallibility and necessity of the Word of God. He spoke against worldliness and hypocrisy among Christians, and against Roman Catholicism, ritualism, and modernism.

One of the biggest controversies in his life was known as the "Down-Grade Controversy." Charles Spurgeon believed that some pastors of his time were "downgrading" the faith by compromising with the world or the new ideas of the age. He said that some pastors were denying the inspiration of the Bible, salvation by faith alone, and the truth of the Bible in other areas, such as creation. Many pastors who believed what Spurgeon condemned were not happy about this, and Spurgeon eventually resigned from the Baptist Union.

Despite some difficulties, Spurgeon became known as the "Prince of Preachers." He opposed slavery, started a pastors' college, opened an orphanage, led in helping feed and clothe the poor, had a book fund for pastors who could not afford books, and more.

Charles Spurgeon remains one of the most published preachers in history. His sermons were printed each week (even in the newspapers), and then the sermons for the year were re-issued as a book at the end of the year. The first six volumes, from 1855-1860, are known as *The Park Street Pulpit*, while the next fifty-seven volumes, from 1861-1917 (his sermons continued to be published long after his death), are known as *The Metropolitan Tabernacle Pulpit*. He also oversaw a monthly magazine-type publication called *The Sword and the Trowel,* and Spurgeon wrote many books, including *Lectures to My Students, All of Grace, Around the Wicket Gate, Advice for Seekers, John Ploughman's Talks, The Soul Winner, Words of Counsel for Christian Workers, Cheque Book of the Bank of Faith, Morning and Evening,* his autobiography, and more, including some commentaries, such as his twenty-year study on the Psalms – *The Treasury of David.*

Charles Spurgeon often preached ten times a week, preaching to an estimated ten million people during his lifetime. He usually preached from only one page of notes, and often from just an outline. He read about six books each week. During his lifetime, he had read *The Pilgrim's Progress* through more than one hundred times. When he died, his personal library consisted of more than 12,000 books. However, the Bible always remained the most important book to him.

Spurgeon was able to do what he did in the power of God's Holy Spirit because he followed his own advice – he met with God every morning before meeting with others, and he continued in communion with God throughout the day.

Charles Spurgeon suffered from gout, rheumatism, and some depression, among other health problems. He often went to Menton, France, to recuperate and rest. He preached his final sermon at the Metropolitan

Tabernacle on June 7, 1891, and died in France on January 31, 1892, at the age of fifty-seven. He was buried in Norwood Cemetery in London.

Charles Haddon Spurgeon lived a life devoted to God. His sermons and writings continue to influence Christians all over the world.

Similar Titles

Jesus Came to Save Sinners
by Charles H. Spurgeon

This is a heart-level conversation with you, the reader. Every excuse, reason, and roadblock for not coming to Christ is examined and duly dealt with. If you think you may be too bad, or if perhaps you really are bad and you sin either openly or behind closed doors, you will discover that life in Christ is for you too. You can reject the message of salvation by faith, or you can choose to live a life of sin after professing faith in Christ, but you cannot change the truth as it is, either for yourself or for others. As such, it behooves you and your family to embrace truth, claim it for your own, and be genuinely set free for now and eternity. Come and embrace this free gift of God, and live a victorious life for Him.

Available where books are sold and free as an eBook

Following Christ, Charles H. Spurgeon

You cannot have Christ if you will not serve Him. If you take Christ, you must take Him in all His qualities. You must not simply take Him as a Friend, but you must also take Him as your Master. If you are to become His disciple, you must also become His servant. God-forbid that anyone fights against that truth. It is certainly one of our greatest delights on earth to serve our Lord, and this is to be our joyful vocation even in heaven itself: *His servants shall serve Him: and they shall see His face* (Revelation 22:3-4).

Available where books are sold and free as an eBook

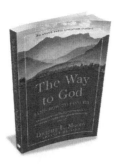

The Way to God, Dwight L. Moody

There is life in Christ. Rich, joyous, wonderful life. It is true that the Lord disciplines those whom He loves and that we are often tempted by the world and our enemy, the devil. But if we know how to go beyond that temptation to cling to the cross of Jesus Christ and keep our eyes on our Lord, our reward both here on earth and in heaven will be 100 times better than what this world has to offer.

This book is thorough. It brings to life the love of God, examines the state of the unsaved individual's soul, and analyzes what took place on the cross for our sins. *The Way to God* takes an honest look at our need to repent and follow Jesus, and gives hope for unending, joyous eternity in heaven.

Available where books are sold and free as an eBook

Absolute Surrender, by Andrew Murray

God waits to bless us in a way beyond what we expect. From the beginning, ear has not heard, neither has the eye seen, what God has prepared for those who wait for Him (Isaiah 64:4). God has prepared unheard of things, things you never can think of, blessings much more wonderful than you can imagine and mightier than you can conceive. They are divine blessings. Oh, come at once and say, "I give myself absolutely to God, to His will, to do only what God wants." God will enable you to carry out the surrender necessary, if you come to Him with a sincere heart.

Available where books are sold and free as an eBook

The Kneeling Christian, by Albert Richardson

Lord Jesus is as powerful today as ever before. The Lord Jesus is as anxious for men to be saved as ever before. His arm is not shortened that it cannot save, but He does stretch forth His arm unless we pray more – and more genuinely. Prayer, real prayer, is the noblest, the sublimest and most stupendous act that any creature of God can perform. Lord, teach us how to pray.

Available where books are sold and free as an eBook

Made in the USA
Coppell, TX
04 October 2023